The Power of Moms with Dreams

Secrets to Help Busy Moms Live Their Dreams, Get Results, and Model Success to Their Children

Includes WORKSHEETS

By
D.A. Batrowny

Copyright © 2019 by Buffdon Publishing. All Rights Reserved.

No part of this publication may be reproduced, distributed, or transmitted in any form or by any means, including photocopying, recording, or other electronic or mechanical methods, or by any information storage and retrieval system without the prior written permission of the publisher, except in the case of very brief quotations embodied in critical reviews and certain other non-commercial uses permitted by copyright law.

The methods describe within this book are the author's personal thoughts. They are not intended to be a definitive set of instructions for this project. You may discover there are other methods and materials to accomplish the same end result.

The author has made every effort to ensure the accuracy of the information within this book was correct at time of publication. The author does not assume and hereby disclaims any liability to any party for any loss, damage, or disruption caused by errors or omissions, whether such errors or omissions result from accident, negligence, or any other cause.

Printed in the United States of America

Preface

The day had finally arrived. I would be meeting with my guidance counselor, Mr. Lenhart, to get the results from the life career test that was given to the seniors. *Now, I thought, I will finally be clear about the direction my life should take.* I remember it vividly. I could barely contain my excitement as Mr. Lenhart slowly opened the manila folder and pulled out my test. Scientist? Marketer? CEO? Where did my strengths lie? As I sat nervously squirming in my chair, he placed the paper on the desk in front of me, smiled, and explained the results showed my strengths were best suited for the nursing and clergy fields.

What? Did I hear him wrong? Was he serious? Was that what I had been waiting for all this time? Was there a mistake? After taking a minute to digest what he said, I asked him why the test selected clergy and nursing as the fields I should pursue. He responded, "Your answers show you like to help people." I was stunned because at the time, I considered the nursing and clergy fields to be the polar opposite of the glamorous career I envisioned.

I laughed as I told my friends the results and then denounced the test as fraudulent. I became determined to prove the results wrong. I was going to become a successful businesswoman!

I had always wanted to be an entrepreneur and run my own exciting business, just like my aunt Kaye. She was a broker and Realtor in the Washington DC area. While growing up, I was in awe of her as she rolled into our small town in her huge Cadillac convertible, wearing Jackie O style sunglasses and a headscarf. I loved to listen to her exciting and inspiring business adventures. Each summer when I visited her, I helped in her office and attended her meetings. We dined on flaming shish kabob at rooftop restaurants and shopped for business suits. She introduced me to fascinating and well-known people. I dreamed of being my own boss so I could not only earn money but also create unique ideas and provide expertise to my customers. I wasn't certain which type of business I would pursue, but I knew it would be exciting and I would love every minute of it. I also knew it wouldn't be in the nursing or clergy fields.

Well, that was just the start of my journey to find my ideal life. I entered college as a business major, but after almost three years, I decided that I needed to earn money right away. A friend pointed out a field that had large demand and good pay, and I had already completed all the required electives.

"That sounds great!" I said. "What is it?"

"Nursing," he replied to my dismay. So, after changing my major and taking a few more courses, I became a registered nurse. Yes, a nurse! That was just one of the many times in my life that I vividly recalled my visit with Mr. Lenhart. There he was again, placing the test in front of me as I sat nervously squirming in my chair. All I could do was shake the memory off and continue on with the new direction of my life.

Well, the money in nursing was good, but the night shift was tiring. I thought once I could get on the day shift, it would be better. I started the day shift, but getting time off was difficult. I couldn't even get time off for my honeymoon! I gave birth to my adorable baby daughter a year later and was able to spend four months at home with her, but leaving her to return to work practically killed me. After spending Thanksgiving and Christmas at work, I knew this was *not* the way I had envisioned our life. I felt guilty for not being able to spend much time with my family and disappointed that I hadn't followed my dream to become an entrepreneur. I finally left that job for another nursing job with less pay and benefits in exchange for weekends and holidays with my family.

When my precious son was born, I was only able to stay home with him for eight weeks. Once I returned to work, the childcare costs for two children consumed most of my salary. I soon realized I would actually bring home more money if I worked part-time, used less daycare and enlisted the help of a relative to care for my children one day a week. I started working part-time, spent more time with my children and thought that everything would be great, but in the back of my mind, I still wanted to be that businesswoman. I completed my business degree by taking night classes, in hopes that someday, when the children were older, I could pursue my dream. At the time, I believed it was impossible to pursue my dream and raise my family at the same time, so I continued to educate myself and returned to college whenever I could to take computer courses.

My part-time nursing job involved working with young parents and their children, providing developmental education and screenings. I really enjoyed all that I was learning about child development and the opportunities I received. I especially loved helping mothers and their families. Over the years, I became a program supervisor, worked in a multi-year world-renowned research project, coordinated a program in one of the first researched school readiness programs that resulted in impressive increases in readiness and became the director of multiple developmental programs for children and families. I was happy with my career and my family, but I still wanted to identify and pursue my passion.

During that time, I became tired of completing the same daily routine and felt exhausted at the end of each day. I was so immersed in the day-to-day tasks of my job and raising my children that I forgot about making time for my dreams and myself. I saw less and less of my friends, felt like I only passed my husband periodically and was drifting further away from all the goals I once had. Several years later, when my confidence took a dive, I decided it was time to make a change.

I started to research online for ideas for a business that interested me, as well as advice on how to create and achieve goals. When I could make time, I began to read books, listen to audio and study online courses related to finding my passion and achieving goals in all areas of my life. While doing this, I discovered other like-minded people who felt the same way and wanted to reach goals related to their own interests, and I connected with them. We helped each other.

I found that much of the information in the courses and books I studied was not geared toward busy moms with very little free time, like me. I knew the information was helpful, but I needed to find a way to create bite-size pieces that would allow me to get the same results without spending much time doing it or becoming exhausted. I analyzed what worked for me, discarded what didn't, tweaked what needed tweaking and focused on refining every step to the optimal, most timely process possible. That is when I became inspired and felt hope that using my new plan would leave me inspired, motivated and allow me to reach my goals much sooner.

I discovered that if I carved out just 15 minutes a day, I could start making small changes that together would create a big impact. I learned that continuous action, even if just for a few minutes each day, could get the ball rolling. I learned that when the ball started rolling, it picked up speed, leading me to the exciting life I had been dreaming about so many years before, sometimes when I least expected it. I discovered that little by little, I could design my ideal life and feel inspired. I discovered that I could face fear and not be defeated. Once I began consistently using this plan, I was able to run my own business, help others reach their goals, develop my interest in writing, travel with my family and enjoy life like never before. But most of all, after years of trial and error, reading countless books, evaluating and refining processes, then putting them into action, I finally realized what my true passion was. And guess who showed up once again? Yes, there he was, Mr. Lenhart! He was once again in my head, placing the test in front of me as I sat nervously squirming in my chair. This time, I finally understood why he was there, so I cherished the moment and smiled.

You see, I finally realized that my true passion is to help people find happiness in their lives, and I discovered that while searching my own life. The process I used helped me understand that I didn't have to be a nurse or part of the clergy, because there were an infinite number of ways I could align my vision to be that businesswoman, live my passion of helping people, and raise my family all at the same time. Once I figured that out, my life fell into place. Mr. Lenhart, the test was right! I just didn't know the process!

From that moment on, I was able to take a look at my life

and my desires and create ambitious goals that I could achieve within my already busy day. I changed. I was happy. I went on to do everything I dreamed of and still am. I have time to enjoy my family and travel. I educate and inspire others to succeed and live the life of their dreams. I am the author of several books, the founder of the Maxi Mom Success System and the founder of World Child Development Day.

Soon, others began noticing my excitement and asking me how I was able to accomplish so much. People told me I inspired them and asked what my secret was. Even though I always thought I enjoyed and lived a happy life, my happiness increased tenfold. I started to share the process with those who asked, and I couldn't contain the happiness I felt while watching them begin to attain their own goals.

I began to consider what would have happened if I had followed this process much earlier, such as when I was in high school or starting a family. It blew my mind to think about the possibilities.

My background in child development took over, and I began to wonder how following this process while raising my young family would have impacted my children. I knew that if children learned these simple concepts on their own level and developed success habits before they even knew there was any other way, it could change their lives forever. Because children learn so much from watching what parents do and not from what parents say, a mother who is modeling this process could contribute to her child's development of positive success habits that could provide benefits for a lifetime. Additionally, if her child was being introduced to a sampling of the concepts in age-appropriate pieces, her child may even develop these success habits *before* entering school. Now imagine the impact that could have. At that moment, I knew I had to start writing immediately. What mother doesn't want to learn an easy process to design her future, find happiness, be successful *and* share some of those same concepts with her children? I know I did.

INTRODUCTION

Here's a mom who really understood many of the concepts included in this book. She was one of six children. She enjoyed writing as a child and even created her own book at a very young age. As she got older, she followed the educational wishes of her parents, but never lost track of her passion.

One day, she came up with an idea to write a story that really excited her. She was so enthusiastic about her project, she decided to quickly take action. She later scheduled time to pursue her goal around her daily activities while also raising her daughter. Although she encountered obstacles along the way, she didn't let them deter her. Instead, she maneuvered around them.

At one point, she required the support of social benefits as a single parent doing the best she could to raise her child. She continued step by step toward her goal and didn't let obstacles, limiting beliefs or lack of experience stop her from reaching it. Even after years of working on her book, she never gave up. She was turned down by multiple publishers and heard typical comments including the difficulties of making money from children's books. She could have told herself that she was not a good enough writer and given up. She could have given up when she began parenting her daughter alone. She could have given up because of the length of time before she would see possible results. But she did not.

She went on to become one of the greatest authors of all time because she decided to succeed and did not let anything stand in the way of her passion and goals. Her book became a series, her series was turned into several movies and best of all, she inspired millions of children to develop a love for reading, including my own! You may already have figured out the author described in this story. Her name is JK Rowling. Imagine if any one of her challenges, thoughts or time constraints caused her to give up, not follow her passion, and never write that first Harry Potter book.

WHY I WROTE THIS BOOK

I wrote this book because I want you to see that you have the potential within you, to not only reach your goals, but to begin designing the life you want to live today. What will make you happy? What do you want your future to be like? What is important to you? What excites you? What will help you wake up every day filled with zest? Whether you want to be an author, entrepreneur, lose 10 pounds, strengthen your relationships or just live a happier more fulfilled life, I want you to know about the simple process you can fit into *your* daily life that will help you discover your passions, live the life of your dreams and help you guide your child toward a wonderful, happy, successful life. The individual steps discussed in each chapter can create positive results, but the results you can obtain when using the entire process can be life-changing. YOU can create the transformational blueprint for your future!

WHY YOU SHOULD READ THIS BOOK

So admit it, balancing life with children is harder than ever. Then, if you throw your work and social life on top of the laundry pile of responsibilities, add a sprinkle of guilt and a bit of regret.... "Wait, what social life?" you may ask. Well, I think you get the picture.

Do you remember the last time you spent a day feeling happy, confident, productive and inspired because you were not only doing what was exciting to you and reaching your own goals, but you were also providing the foundation for a successful future, including lifelong benefits for your child?

In this book, I will show you how to design the life you want to live in the time you have to give. As you work through the book, you will discover tips to feel happier, raise your confidence as an individual and a parent, create your own success, feel proud of yourself, explore your passions and interests, cut through chaos, stretch available time, find new resources, extend your own knowledge and provide a great foundation for your child. The best part is that you will enjoy instant results with some of the techniques. Others will require a consistent continual effort, but the results are worth it! The tips you will learn, when used successfully, will create lifelong habits and unbelievable results that together, can totally transform the way you view and live your life.

Parents who once struggled with day-to-day responsibilities leaving little time for their own goals, and limited quality time with their children, have already used the methods provided in this book with great success.

Sarah was busy working full-time while trying to raise her children and make sure there was money to pay the bills. She was working in a fast food restaurant and came home tired every day. Her schedule changed often, and she missed many of her children's school events. She felt like she would never be able to make a change because there was never much time left after working and completing household chores.

One day when she was asking me about one of my new ventures, she told me that her dream was to work from home so she could spend more time with her children, but she said she knew that was impossible. When I followed up on her comment, she explained that she didn't have any skills to make money from home and could never just quit her job. We started talking about designing her future, and after using the worksheets and process in this book, she was able to identify her passion for taking photos, create goals and break them down into a step-by-step plan that she started working on for 15 minutes after the children went to bed each night. She became so excited about realizing her dream that she decided to also use her lunch breaks and travel time to gain more knowledge and complete other small tasks that propelled her to ultimately reach her goal. When she had her carefully designed plan in place, she gradually made the transition from fast food to photography. She currently runs a small business as a photographer, enjoys more quality time with her children and loves what she does. She has witnessed the benefits to her family, her career and her confidence level.

I promise you that if you read this book and successfully master the simple tips provided, you will double or triple your productivity and decrease your daily stressors. You will have time to enjoy the stages of your child's development, feel more at ease, and have a different outlook on life altogether, but the best part is that your child will also reap rewards, by developing positive habits that will be of benefit for a lifetime.

Don't be the person who reads the book and says, "I'll do this later when I have more time or when the kids are older." That time may never come. As your child grows, life gets more complicated, and the tips in this book will be much easier and more beneficial to start today. I'll even show you how to find the time in your very busy day. The longer you wait, the greater the chance that some of the things you do every day, that you may not even realize are negatively impacting your child, may soon become the same habits your child develops and begins to use over and over again. If you don't do it for you, do it for your child, and I promise you will both feel the results!

The book is organized so that it is easy to complete the entire process by focusing on one step at a time. Each chapter also contains a bonus section detailing specific ideas of how to present a sampling of some of the same material to your child in an age-appropriate way. There are handy chapter reviews and helpful worksheets for you and end-of-chapter exercises to help you and your child. This book is made so you can return to it over and over again as you continue to design and refine your amazing life plan.

Read this book and take action now, and *I promise*, you won't regret it! The tips in this book were obtained after years of trial and error, studying, reading countless books and evaluating processes. Learning one or two of the many tips will benefit you in life, but your success will multiply when you take action in all the areas discussed in the book, creating a plan for your future success. Imagine a hot air balloon that is not completely filled. You could get in it and it may still float above the ground, but it would risk hitting taller objects, and the view would not be as great. If the hot air balloon was full, it would easily soar high up in the air above the obstacles, and the view would be breathtaking. If you're going to make this commitment, take all the steps so you will soar and have plenty of time to enjoy the magnificent view!

THIS BOOK WILL HELP YOU...

learn to become more positive, develop clarity about what you want in life, feel more confident, plan and reach your goals, save time, understand why saying no can be a good thing, knock down your fears, find out how to fit free learning into a hectic day, find others who want to help and support you, teach your child success habits, and much, much more! So, let's get started!

HOW TO USE THIS BOOK

Although there are many ways to use this book, the recommended process includes reading each chapter, completing the worksheets and exercises at the end of each chapter, and taking the time to practice each skill or task before moving on to the next chapter. People will pass through this process a bit differently depending on their own unique situation, their available time and where they are in the process when they start reading the book.

As you move through the book, if you feel you have *not* mastered a previous skill, return to the chapter that addresses that skill and either start reading again from that point or just reread that chapter and practice the related skills, then return to where you left off. Base your decision on whether your clarity about that skill affected your understanding of the topics discussed following that chapter.

Once you have completed the book, you are not done! You will want to use the book as a guide and return to it often as you refine your goals, confront obstacles, review topics, need inspiration, want to reread the information that wasn't relevant when you started, or are ready to move on to another goal after successfully completing the one you were working on. Once you start reading you will discover the manner that works best for you as you begin to understand, practice and master the concepts in this book. Are you ready?

CONTENTS

PREFACE i
INTRODUCTION vii

CHAPTER 1: BOOST YOUR POSITIVITY 1
HOW POSITIVITY HELPS YOUR CHILD 9
BOOST YOUR POSITIVITY REVIEW 13
Boost Your Positivity Exercises 13
Boost Your Positivity Exercises to Help Your Child 14

CHAPTER 2: LOOK INSIDE 17
HOW LOOKING INSIDE HELPS YOUR CHILD 24
LOOK INSIDE REVIEW 27
Look Inside Exercises 27
Look Inside Exercises to Help Your Child 28

**CHAPTER 3: EXPLORE YOUR PASSIONS
AND DESIRES** 31
HOW EXPLORING PASSIONS AND DESIRES
HELPS YOUR CHILD 38
EXPLORE YOUR PASSIONS AND DESIRES REVIEW 43
Explore Your Passions and Desires Exercises 43
Explore Your Passions and Desires Exercises
to Help Your Child 44

CHAPTER 4: BELIEVE IN YOURSELF 47
HOW BELIEVING IN YOURSELF HELPS YOUR CHILD 54
BELIEVE IN YOURSELF REVIEW 59
Believe in Yourself Exercises 59
Believe in Yourself Exercises to Help Your Child 60

CHAPTER 5: GET STARTED 63
HOW GETTING STARTED HELPS YOUR CHILD 71
GET STARTED REVIEW 75
Get Started Exercises... 76
Get Started Exercises to Help Your Child 77

CHAPTER 6: FIND TIME 81
HOW FINDING TIME HELPS YOUR CHILD 90
FIND TIME REVIEW 93
Find Time Exercises.. 93
Find Time Exercises to Help Your Child 95

CHAPTER 7: GET ORGANIZED 99
HOW GETTING ORGANIZED HELPS YOUR CHILD 106
GET ORGANIZED REVIEW 110
Get Organized Exercises 110
Get Organized Exercises to Help Your Child 111

CHAPTER 8: CONQUER FEAR! 117
HOW CONQUERING FEAR HELPS YOUR CHILD 129
CONQUER FEAR CHAPTER REVIEW 134
Conquer Fear Exercises... 135
Conquer Fear Exercises to Help Your Child 136

CHAPTER 9: LEARN TO LOVE LEARNING 139
HOW LEARNING TO LOVE LEARNING
HELPS YOUR CHILD 147
LEARN TO LOVE LEARNING REVIEW 152
Learn to Love Learning Exercises............................... 153
Learn to Love Learning Exercises to Help Your Child 154

CHAPTER 10: GRAB YOUR BONUS
TIPS AND TOOLS 159
HOW GRABBING YOUR BONUS TIPS
AND TOOLS HELPS YOUR CHILD 170
GRAB YOUR BONUS TIPS AND TOOLS REVIEW 174

Grab Your Bonus Tips and Tools Exercises 175
Grab Your Bonus Tips and Tools Exercises
to Help Your Child 176

CHAPTER 11: CELEBRATE THE NEW YOU 183

HOW CELEBRATING THE NEW YOU
HELPS YOUR CHILD 189

CELEBRATE THE NEW YOU REVIEW 192
Celebrate the New You Exercises 193
Celebrate the New You Exercises to Help Your Child 193

FROM ME TO YOU: 199
ABOUT THE AUTHOR 200

CHAPTER 1

BOOST YOUR POSITIVITY

CAN YOU RELATE?

Wow, what a hectic day it's been. You sit down, or should I say collapse, into the chair, so happy the baby finally fell asleep. Then suddenly, you feel something soft and lumpy directly beneath you. You shoot back out of the chair faster than a lightning bolt, fearing that you just sat on the cat. Luckily, it only turns out to be the clean laundry you threw down earlier when you noticed your dog's tail start to smoke as he was sitting too close to the fireplace! You toss the clothes on the floor and fall back into the chair. You finally feel your muscles begin to relax, and you start to close your eyes. As you lower your eyes, you think, *I really have to stop wearing these pants every day!* You then notice and scrape what you hope is pureed squash off your arm. Just then, the dog decides to bark at a squirrel in the yard, waking the baby from her lovely 3-minute sleep, and you're back at it again!

I certainly can relate to days like that. I remember one day when I thought I had it all together and was so proud of myself because I was able to get both children to nap and was able to clean the house at the same time. As the dog and both children slept peacefully, I thought, *Oh the house is clean and the children are asleep. I can actually rest and enjoy these few precious moments of motherhood.* I then walked into the kitchen to get a drink, noticed cereal pieces on the floor behind the stove, and for some crazy reason, decided to move the stove to get them. The gas pipe broke and I could hear the gas hissing out into the air. Not sure where to turn off the gas, I went to the phone and called 911. I quietly said, "My gas stove pipe broke and I do not need a fire truck, but could you please just tell me how to turn off the gas?" I immediately heard the fire whistle at the nearby fire station sound and a few minutes later, my street was blocked off at both ends. My children were taken safely across the street, my neighbor was hammering on my freshly painted and stuck windows to try to open them, and the firemen could not find the gas turn-off valve!

Needless to say, I made it through that day, and when my husband arrived home to see his wife and rested children happily playing in a thoroughly cleaned house, the first thing he said was, "Wow, you would not believe the day I had!"

I said, "I don't think it could have been as bad as mine."

He said, "I think it was."

After several times back and forth with this conversation, he smugly told me to go first, and before I was even done with my story, he said, "You win!" We still laugh about that day, and our children have heard the story told many times!

Moms often fearlessly (or fearfully in that case), handle everything. Let's look a little closer. If you're a parent, you already have skills that might make a corporate worker cringe. Have you ever made dinner while taking care of a sick baby, feeding the dog, doing laundry and distracting your toddler at the same time? Well, as parents, we do what we need to do without giving it a second thought. We handle unexpected gas leaks and leaking children. We multitask like the best of them. We plan, organize and plot our next move. We take action, reorganize and try it again. We handle unhappy children and uncooperative children. We learn new tricks, think on our toes and invent new ways of doing things. We convince the angriest toddler why pants and underwear must be worn at the grocery store, all while wearing a smile. Those are exactly the skills that are needed to succeed in any endeavor. You are already highly qualified for life and for any job you desire!

Being a parent can be frustrating to say the least, and whether you are deep in the middle of peeling a dirty diaper off the bottom of your bare foot or sprinting out of your house with your children in tow just in case it explodes, there is one major thing besides a sense of humor that can make things better. That thing is positivity.

Focus on the positive.
Positivity means knowing there may be days like the ones just described, but not forgetting there are two ways of looking at things. It's simple. You can focus on the positive or focus on the negative.

Let's take the first example of the hectic day. Here's a completely different way to look at it. You finally get the baby to sleep. You plop down in the chair and feel something soft and lumpy under you. You laugh when you realize it is not the cat, as you first thought, but just a pile of clothes you put there earlier when you thought the dog was on fire. You laugh again. You sit back down, thankful that your laundry is clean so that it can be folded when there is time. It is not an emergency, so doing it at a later time won't matter. You have a warm home, a soft chair and a safe place to raise your child. You were fortunate to have spent an entire day playing, reading, and lovingly interacting with your child. You helped promote your child's development and pre-literacy skills. You saw her roll on the floor as she used her problem-solving skills to try to get the toy you placed just out of her reach. She smiled at you and grabbed at the book you read to her, and when you fed her, she gazed in your eyes and smiled. You are able to take care of your pets and provide love to them too. Just then, the dog barks and wakes up the baby. You think about what a great watch dog you have. The baby's crying, because she needs you and it is great that she has you to depend on. Being able to depend on you teaches trust, which is an important concept for your child to learn because it will impact relationships she builds in the future. The things you did today really mattered and can impact your child for years to come. It was a wonderful day!

If you practice the positivity tips listed in this chapter every day, you will notice a big change in the way you feel. You may have even felt a bit of that feeling as you read the last paragraph. This change will be the first simple step in a process that will take you to a happy life that you will love!

Play the goodness game.
This is something I love to do that is fun and can actually change the way you view life. You can start becoming more positive by playing a game that I call the "goodness game." Throughout the day, look for all that is positive around you. Look for positive outcomes, smiles, positive statements, good deeds, and even unintended goodness as a result of any action of others! Examples could be someone holding the door for you as you enter the grocery store, a police officer directing traffic, a man petting his dog or even a smile from someone you pass. Make it a fun game and keep score by earning one point for each positive thing you notice. I will warn you that as you become more in tune with goodness instead of negativity, you will notice so many positive things, you will have a difficult time keeping a mental tally, so don't forget to bring along your phone or a pen to keep track! Try to increase your score each day and notice how you begin to identify more and more goodness around you.

Find the good in a bad situation.
Another way to find goodness is to ask, "What good do I see here?" Do this every time you think a negative thought or experience a negative situation. If you look closely enough, you can always find something that is good in just about anything. For instance, if you walked into your freezing cold kitchen on a snowy morning and found the back door wide open because your child let the dog out into the fenced yard and forgot to shut the door, look for the positive in the situation instead of getting upset. In this example, you could be grateful that your child helped out and you didn't have to clean up the dog's mess on the floor, and you didn't end up being late for work.

An example from my own life happened right before my mother died of cancer. She was a strong woman but became very weak in her last days of life. The day before she died, she smiled and called me over to her chair. When I got there, she looked up, smiled and said with awe, "Look at the stars. Aren't they beautiful?" It was a moment I will never forget. Since that day, I've seen many quotes that mention that without the darkness, it's impossible to see the stars, and I've looked up at the sky on a starry night and felt that wonderful moment over and over again. Each time I gaze up at the stars, I can choose to be reminded of my mother's unfortunate death or the beauty in her life. I choose to create a happy memory that provides comfort and reminds me to look for the beauty that surrounds me.

You can make the choice to perceive things by looking for the good in them. Use the *Find the Good Worksheet* at the end of the chapter as a guide to help you take the steps to finding the good in a bad situation. This worksheet will guide you as you list difficult situations you have experienced, and then brainstorm until you find something good about that experience, no matter how small it may be.

You may find this difficult to do at first, but it will get easier and easier the longer you do it, until you develop what I call the "happiness habit." As you master the happiness habit, the number of good things you notice will outweigh the negative, until it becomes so natural that you no longer give it a second thought.

Make positive emotions contagious.
When you get to the point where you are identifying increasing goodness, you will begin to notice how much time other people dwell on negative events instead of focusing on the good experiences, even if you've never noticed before. You will also begin to notice how one person discussing a negative experience can impact those around them, by drawing them into the same negative frame of mind, even when they started out happy. Have you ever been in a room when another person's conversation is bringing the whole room down? It can happen very quickly.

Well, you also need to know that it works both ways. If you discuss a positive experience, it can create positivity in others. This concept of emotions being shared has been studied and written about for many years. The University of California-San Francisco, Oregon State University and the University of Jyvaskyla in Finland conducted some of the more recent research.

I personally experienced contagious emotions at a school choir meeting I attended. The discussion was focused on how the choir students would raise the funds for their trip. When the first idea, a carnival, was explained, one of the parents spoke up and detailed a horrible experience she once had while working at a past school carnival. She was very negative and talked at great lengths about her experience. The next person added his own bad experience from working at a carnival fundraiser, and before long, many of the attendees had voiced their own negative stories about carnival fundraisers. As the stories progressed, I could feel the heaviness in the room. People's faces were drawn and many people sat slumped in their chairs. I noticed that no one was trying to brainstorm positive ways to raise funds but were instead sharing every negative experience they could recall, almost as if they were in a contest to tell the worst carnival story ever. As I was just about to point this out in the most delicate way possible, a mom who was late to the meeting rushed in the room. She said she didn't want to interrupt any more than she already had, by being late, then added that she had a great idea and asked if she could share it when the current discussion was complete. As she said this, she was smiling ear to ear, appeared very excited and walked to her chair with a bounce. I couldn't wait to hear it. One of the moms told her she might as well share her idea right then, because the meeting wasn't going anywhere. The late mom shared her idea with great enthusiasm, and what she didn't know was that it was exactly what was discussed before she came in: a carnival fundraiser. She went on and on discussing the details with great excitement in her voice and then, another mom was smiling and nodding, then another, and soon all the parents at the meeting were visibly excited about having a carnival. I sat dumbfounded but happy that everyone was being so positive and I didn't have to speak up. One person changed the mood of the room and the emotional direction of the others. Before the meeting ended, we voted unanimously on having a carnival fundraiser. The carnival ended up being a big success and the kids raised enough money for a great trip.

If you would like to experience contagious emotions, try getting very excited and sharing a positive story with others and watch what happens to those you are talking to. They may get excited or even share a positive story in return. If you are really interested in putting this to the test even further, try telling a very exciting positive story, after one or more people share a negative or complaining story. I have tried this on many occasions and have been able to completely change the vibe in the room. It really works.

When you master looking for and sharing the positive in your daily life, you will find that you feel happier, lighter, less stressed, and you may even notice that others around you are positively affected. So, take a minute right now, look around you and start spreading positive emotion!

Put gratitude in your attitude.
One of the best ways to feel better instantly is to be grateful. To me, there is nothing in the world better than feeling grateful. Even when I am having a setback, if I focus on what I am grateful for, I can quickly feel my emotions turn around. I feel calmer and more peaceful. I have so much to be grateful for. I have a roof over my head. I have children and family who love me. I have food. I have health. Sometimes, I may not have all the things I want, but I can always find something to be thankful for.

The secret is that no matter how bad a situation may be, there is usually something you can find to be grateful about. You have probably seen this before while watching the news. A family member loses all their possessions in a fire or flood, but during the interview, they explain how grateful they are that their family was not harmed. Hopefully, you will not experience such an extreme situation, but consistently thinking in this manner will train your mind to look past the negative and find the positive aspects of a situation. At times, I have had to look a bit harder to find the goodness, and sometimes, it may not hit me until a few days or weeks later, but if I ask myself what is good about the situation, I can almost always find the goodness.

When I supervised a nursing group that worked with parents of newborns, I found that we often started our staff meetings full of energy and left quiet and mellow after discussing some of the more difficult topics during each meeting. After pointing this out at the end of one of our meetings, we wanted to find something to be grateful for to turn our feelings around. We decided to look at the newborn's photos on our local hospital's website and soon, we were happy and laughing and even ended up staying through part of our lunch break to look at them. The next week, I added a new topic to the end of our agenda and called it "good things that happened this week." After that, we were more likely to leave the meetings feeling a bit happier.

Another trick to redirect your emotions is to place a reminder to be grateful in your phone calendar and set it for a twice-daily reminder. That really works for me. Even when I'm busy, I set alerts on my phone that force me to take a minute to remember all that I have to be grateful for. There have even been times when I was in the middle of something very frustrating and "be grateful" popped up on my phone. That caused me to realize my current frustration was not as large as it seemed, and it instantly lifted my mood.

You can also put notes around your house to remind you to be grateful, use the word or an image of gratitude as the screen saver on your phone or computer, put a sign on your refrigerator or bathroom mirror, or carry a card or a special item in your pocket as a reminder to be grateful. Thinking about how grateful you are for a minute before you go to bed, and right before getting out of bed in the morning, can also be a great way to start and end your day feeling good. There are also many free gratitude apps you can download and use on your phone to encourage gratitude such as Grateful and Day One Journal.

Many people use gratitude lists and gratitude journals to increase their gratitude. A very powerful way to feel grateful includes making a gratitude list. You can do this by filling in the *Daily Gratitude Journal Worksheet* at the end of the chapter. After filling out what you are grateful for in all areas of your life, read it over slowly and really experience what you have written with all your senses and emotions, and you will instantly notice how much better you feel. Feel free to repeat this task daily in a notebook, on your phone or computer, or reread your worksheet each day to increase your daily gratitude.

Try out and select the gratitude tips that work for you and combine as many as you can for additional results. Use them at least once or twice a day, and start feeling the results.

HOW POSITIVITY HELPS YOUR CHILD

I didn't think my childhood was any different than that of many of my friends. I played outside, went on a yearly vacation, and attended Sunday school. One day, I was talking to a friend who was telling me about an acquaintance of hers who told her that she had experienced a "terrible childhood." This friend was blaming her present life situation on her childhood. As I listened to my friend speak, I was stunned. Many of the "terrible" things her friend was saying had happened during her childhood had also happened to me, yet I never viewed my life as "terrible." I always believed I had a great childhood. I thought about this for days. I wondered why two people could react so differently to such similar situations.

Let me tell you a bit about my childhood. When I was seven years old, my father received a severe traumatic brain injury in an automobile accident. At that time, the doctors said that if he lived, the best place for him was in a nursing home because they felt he would have to learn all his skills over again and would never be independent. After much convincing and promising, my mother finally was able to get the doctors to agree to let my father come home. She spent many hours teaching my father simple activities like using eating utensils and walking. There were emergency calls when he would experience a seizure, and for quite a while after his injury, we had to keep the doors locked so he would not wander out of the house on his own.

So, let me tell you why I always felt that I had a happy childhood. My mother's actions set the tone. My mother was positive. She did not complain about our circumstances. She continued to keep positive about life and always viewed the bright side of things. She focused on the fact that we still had our father with us. She found support through family and church. Since my mother needed to stay home with my father, money was tight, yet we still went on vacation every year to visit our cousins, which included a trip to the nearby seashore. We didn't have every toy and item we wanted, but when the topic came up, she explained that we just didn't have the money, and I accepted that. I have wonderful memories of my youth, and I never focused on the negative because my mother's positive approach really changed the entire way I viewed my circumstances. She didn't blame anyone for the past, and she took control of the future. As I became a mother with my own children, I realized how difficult that time must have been for my mother, and I still marvel at how she was able to stay positive and model such great messages to her children.

Now, you might ask how does my positivity and happiness relate to my baby or child? Let me tell you how. Being positive and looking at the bright side of things, instead of complaining and blaming, will make you a much happier person. This will decrease your stress level and make you more relaxed, as you greatly decrease the amount of time you are uptight. This happens as a result of reacting to situations more positively.

Remember the example earlier in this chapter when the mom was finally attempting to rest in the chair after getting the baby to sleep following her long exhausting day? The first version of the story produced a lot of stress for the mother. The second version, which included the mother feeling grateful for spending quality time with her child even though she was exhausted, made her feel calmer and less stressful. It can work in just about any situation. Which mother would you say was more capable of lovingly comforting her crying baby?

Reduce stress for you and your child.
It's important to know that stress affects babies and children in many ways, especially during the first several years of development. That is why one of the greatest tips to calm an upset baby, which has been provided by professionals for years, is to have the mother hold the baby in her arms and sing a calm song.

This works because when a mom is holding a baby who won't calm down, she typically tenses up her muscles and the baby can feel this. The mother's singing relaxes her tense muscles; the baby feels the mother relax and starts to relax too. Have you ever tried to sing a calm song and feel angry at the same time? Try it right now. Try to be angry and at the same time sing a slow, sweet song. It's very difficult to do, isn't it? That is why singing a lullaby can help a very tired, frustrated mom control her body and feelings when she may find it difficult to do so. This can work in the same way that thinking thoughts of gratitude can benefit you when you are feeling down. Try using either technique when in any negative situation and experience the effects for yourself. These tips are very helpful, but please do remember that even the best mothers can get overtired and highly stressed, so if you are ever past the point of calming down, always place your baby in a safe place until you can compose yourself or get help.

Play the goodness game with your child.
When your child becomes more positive, your child will be happier. One way to teach your child to be positive is to teach them the goodness game and play it with them. While driving in the car or taking a walk, see who can point out the most positive things observed along the way. Remember that some examples may include a mother helping her baby, a driver letting a pedestrian cross the street, a pet owner walking his dog, and a woman sweeping a sidewalk. Even younger children can play the game by counting smiles or saying the word "smile" every time they see someone smiling when riding in a car or taking a shopping trip. It can be a fun way to point out positivity. This technique can even be used if a child happens to observe a tragic

news event on TV. Explain that at times, unfortunate things happen, but often when something like that happens, many people do good things to help out. Ask the child what positive things they noticed in the story, such as volunteers helping the victims or the police officer saving someone in a fire.

Help your child find the positive in a situation.
When your child experiences a negative situation, for example, the cancellation of a baseball game due to rain or a riding accident that damaged their bike, teach them to ask the question, "What good do I see here?" so they can see that often, there are good things that come out of bad situations. For the cancelled ball game example, it could be they ended up being able to play at a friend's house or they discovered a new movie they enjoyed. For the riding accident example, it could be they didn't get injured and are now more aware of the dangers of the intersection they were riding in. There is almost always good in every situation, even if sometimes it requires reflecting on a situation a while after it happens.

Spread your positive emotions to your child.
The research regarding contagious emotions, mentioned earlier in this chapter, can also play a part in how your baby or child responds, so the more positive and happy you are, the less stressed you will be, and those emotions will be spread to others near you, especially to your children. This has been found to not only work with babies, but also with older children and adults. Happy moms result in happy children.

Teach your child about gratitude.
Explain to your child there is so much to be grateful for, even when things don't always go their way. Provide examples of everyday things that people often take for granted and ask them to come up with examples too. Show your child how to express their own gratitude by drawing, listing or journaling what they are grateful for. Share the *Daily Gratitude Journal Worksheet* or a notebook or journal with an older child.

BOOST YOUR POSITIVITY REVIEW

1. Practicing the positivity tips in this chapter every day will help you feel happier and calmer.
2. Playing the goodness game is a great way to notice all that is positive around you.
3. If you look closely, you can always find something good in almost every situation. At times, it may require reflecting on the situation at a later date.
4. Take advantage of contagious, positive emotions.
5. Remember to be grateful every day so you can live a happier, less stressful life.

Boost Your Positivity Exercises

1. Make a mental or written list of everything that is positive in your life.
2. Make a mental or written list of the positive events that happen each day.
3. Play the goodness game by yourself or with someone else as you go about your day.
4. Fill out the *Find the Good Worksheet* to guide you as you identify the good in difficult situations.
5. Practice creating contagious positive emotions.
6. Fill out the *Daily Gratitude Journal Worksheet* and include 10 things you are grateful for. Make this a daily practice.
7. Set a twice-daily gratitude reminder on your phone.
8. Create other reminders to be grateful such as sticky notes, signs, screensavers, etc., and take at least one minute to be grateful when you observe them.
9. Feel grateful that by being positive, both you and your child will benefit.

Boost Your Positivity Exercises to Help Your Child

1. Play the goodness game with your child.
2. When your child encounters a negative situation, ask your child, "What good do you see here?" and help your child find something good about the situation.
3. Model positivity throughout your day so your child catches the emotions!
4. Discuss gratitude with your child and show your child how to express their gratitude by drawing things, making a list or journaling about what they are grateful for.

FIND THE GOOD WORKSHEET

List your difficulty, brainstorm to find something good about it no matter how small it may be, then decide how it may benefit you or someone else. Return to column three after more reflection, if needed.

Difficulty	What is something good about this?	How will this benefit me/ someone?
EXAMPLE My child left the kitchen door open in the middle of winter.	He did it while trying to help the dog get outside to go to the bathroom.	The dog was able to go to the bathroom, and I did not have to clean a mess or be late for work.

Always search for the good in a bad situation.

DAILY GRATITUDE JOURNAL WORKSHEET

Make a list of 10 things you are grateful for in all areas of your life.

I am grateful for
I am grateful for
I am grateful for
I am grateful for
I am grateful for
I am grateful for
I am grateful for
I am grateful for
I am grateful for
I am grateful for

Now that you have documented what you are grateful for, say thank you from the bottom of your heart, feel it and remember the peaceful feeling as you go throughout your day.

CHAPTER 2

LOOK INSIDE

LEARN ABOUT YOURSELF

Ok, so you're practicing positivity by playing the happiness game, finding the good in negative situations and being grateful. That's great! You're also starting to notice how emotions can be contagious from one person to another, and you are using this knowledge to stay away from negativity and to spread positivity. Now that you are aware of your environment and of others around you, it is time to look deeper inside of you to learn more about yourself and how you think. What are you all about? How do you respond to things that don't go well? What makes you happy? What do you really want?

Take control.
Control is something you probably don't think about constantly as your flying through your busy day, but it can affect the way you feel and view life. You may experience days or situations when you feel totally out of control. I remember feeling the same way but I didn't have to feel that way, and neither do you. You can turn the way you feel completely around by taking greater control of your life. So, it is time to find out how to start feeling great by realizing you are in control of your life and anything is possible. To be in control, the first thing you need to do is to take full responsibility for your feelings and actions. By taking full responsibility for your feelings and actions and not making excuses or blaming other people or circumstances, you can be in complete control of your life! It is not the traffic that makes you late for work all the time. You could leave sooner each day to ensure you start work on time. You may arrive early at times, but

that is ok. It is not your boss who puts you in a bad mood every day. You choose how you react to your boss, and you can choose to be happy and not let him get to you. It is not the stress that makes you binge-eat chips. It's the unhealthy outlet you are choosing to use to deal with your stress. You have the power to change that. You are the only one who is responsible for yourself and your life, so make a commitment right now to stop blaming other people or circumstances and take responsibility.

Everyone has different experiences in life, but you are the one who can decide how to react to them and how to move forward. Have you ever heard the saying, "It's not what happens to you, but how you react to it that determines how you feel"? Keep that in mind when you say, "I can't do this because... I would but... If it wasn't for...". You *can* do whatever you want to do; don't let anyone tell you otherwise.

You have probably heard stories of people who were able to successfully recover from unbelievable tragedies when others could not. Why do you think that is? Attitude and beliefs play a big part. Often, those who succeed decide they want to move forward, feel they deserve to be happy and don't want the event to control the rest of their life. It doesn't mean they have forgotten, but they have decided to take back the control and move forward in a positive manner. They may also try to benefit from anything they learned from the terrible experience.

Take a look at your own situation and ask yourself what steps you need to take to move forward and what beliefs you need to change; then, step by step, start moving. If you don't know how to get started, keep reading. The information in this book will help you do that. Do you want to go back to school but don't think you have time now that you have a baby? Do you want to move past that bad relationship and be happy again? Do you want to feel confident and proud of yourself? Do you want to stay home with your baby but don't think you can because you need to go back to your job or find a job? Do you wish you were skilled in something that would allow you to work for yourself?

You can do anything you want to once you believe in yourself and stop making excuses. If you really want to do something, you *can* do it. I know you can. I will show you how to get started, but the first thing you have to do is take 100 percent responsibility for yourself and get rid of *all* excuses. You may catch yourself making excuses even after you decide to take full responsibility, but that is ok, because now that you are more aware, it will get easier. Don't worry about perceived obstacles because there are ways to get around them, and we will talk about that in detail in chapter four.

Once you take 100 percent responsibility and understand that everything you do relies on you alone, the sky is the limit. You will feel much more positive and powerful, and you will know that the future is up to you and no one else. You don't have to know how to accomplish what you want to do at this point. You only need to know that you alone are responsible for taking the first steps to do this. The *I'm in Control Worksheet* at the end of this chapter will help you list and evaluate your excuses and find solutions so you can take the wheel and steer your life in a positive direction. First, you will brainstorm and then list all the excuses you tell yourself. When you complete the worksheet, it is important to fill out the Excuse Column all the way down the page before starting the other column, so don't skip ahead. When you fill out the Excuse Column, don't give the reason behind each excuse too much thought; quickly jot down the excuses you tell yourself or others when you think or talk about why you haven't done something you had hoped to do. It can be in any area of your life, no matter how big or small you think it may be. When you complete the last column, you will discover ways you can take more control of each situation and your life. If you have trouble with the last column, it may help to take time to think about it. Come back to it more than once if you have to, as you brainstorm more ways to tackle the issue and get to the heart of why you have been thinking the way you have and how to address it.

Figure out what makes you happy.
Now that you have started to look inside and have decided to take full responsibility for your life, it's time to take another peek to figure out what really makes you happy. Take a few minutes to think about what you really enjoy, as well as specific instances in your life when you were the happiest. It could be happy experiences from when you were a young adult, a very young child, yesterday or the great experiences you hope to have in five to ten years. What were/are you doing? Why were/are you so happy? Who were/are you with at the time?

Write these occurrences down using the *Happy Hunting Worksheet* at the end of the chapter. Fill out the columns asking where you were and whom you were with. Once you have filled out the worksheet, look for the common elements. Was it always related to something specific such as music, being around others or being alone in a special place? Was it when you were helping someone, creating something, or planning something? Pay close attention to the Who Column of your worksheet. Were you alone? Were you with others? If so, who was it? Was it always one person? Was it different people, and if so, do they have something in common? At first, it may be difficult to recall those special moments because you may not have thought about some of them since they happened. So, if you think about it for a few days, you will probably remember other happy moments in your life that you may have completely forgotten about. If you can't think of anything at the moment, spend the next few days noticing when you are happiest throughout the day. This worksheet will help you uncover the recurring themes that bring you happiness so you can incorporate them into the plans for your ideal life.

Another way to complete this exercise is to close your eyes and visualize yourself relaxing under a towering shade tree on a beautiful, warm, sunny day. Feel the soft warm breeze on your face, get totally relaxed and relive the great memories from your past, and then think about your hopes and dreams for your future. Get lost in the moments, smell the leaves, hear the birds, feel the happiness bubbling up inside of you as you relive those great moments from your past and fast forward to the happiness in your future.

When I was older and finally looked back over my life, I found that one of the themes I identified included many happy experiences spent helping other people. Remember Mr. Lenhart from the story of my high school career test in the preface of this book? Well, there he was again! As a very young child, I loved to play school and pretend I was teaching the children. I used to play school for hours each day with my pretend students. I had a small chalkboard and would have chalk dust on the floor, on the wall and sometimes on my nose by the end of the day. When I was older, I organized bike clubs and fan clubs in our basement for my neighborhood friends and showed them how to plan bike trips and find the addresses of celebrities. I loved planning the exciting new lesson I would teach each week at our club meetings. Later, I enjoyed teaching some of my friends how to ice skate and speed skate on the local pond, and I helped my girlfriend learn how to drive a car. I volunteered at my children's schools and still love to help and inspire my own children. My career included helping parents with new babies, and I continue helping people to this day. As I looked into some of my dreams for the future, this theme continued.

Now it's time to pick a relaxing spot to visualize in, grab your pen and fill out the *Happy Hunting Worksheet* at the end of the chapter to help you explore some of the underlying themes that create your happiness.

Be clear about what you want.
How many times have you been asked something and your answer was, "I don't care," "I don't know," or "It doesn't matter"? Sometimes, you may be tired or don't want to take the time to consider the option, feel it is not a big deal or think you will appear selfish. After a while it can then become a habit that you don't give any thought to at all. It's time to get clear on what you want. When someone gives you a choice, really think about it and answer honestly. Start by making simple decisions when given the

choice, such as going out to dinner or attending a movie, eating a strawberry ice cream cone or a chocolate ice cream cone, or spending a day at the lake or the ocean. If you really think about the choice, you most likely have a preference, and you deserve to select the choice that makes you the happiest. If you have trouble making a simple choice, quickly consider each decision then pick the one you think will provide the best results, increase your happiness, get you closer to your goal, improve the way you are feeling, or provide a better outcome.

I visited my aunt in Virginia every summer when I was young. At the time, she was a very successful businesswoman. One evening, we were going out to dinner and she gave me two choices and asked me which I preferred. I remember answering, "I don't care," and she responded by saying, "You do care. Now, which do you prefer?" Her response stunned me at first, but after I thought about it, I realized I did have a preference. Thinking back, this was just one of the success tips that she lived by, which contributed to her great success. She was sure about what she wanted and what made her happy. When given the opportunity to do what made her happiest, she embraced it!

So, the next time someone asks you a similar question, think it over, answer confidently and thank them for asking. They wouldn't have asked if they didn't want to know your answer. As I began to do this myself, I became a little clearer about myself. I began to notice that it became easier to make decisions related to my goals. The clearer I became, the easier it was to decide if an action or decision I was making was taking me on the correct path to my own dreams. I was no longer the person who "didn't care," and I became much more confident with each decision I made.

No matter where you are in the process of gaining clarity, I want you to start small and focus on what you really want before moving on to bigger decisions. Then, when you get to the point where you are making bigger decisions, ask yourself, "What makes me know I'm headed in the right direction?" I'm talking about the direction you want to travel, not the direction you or others think you should travel.

Making decisions that can impact you or someone else in any way requires thought. Some decisions require a little thought and some require more. You don't want to go overboard and stress needlessly about making minor decisions, but larger decisions require more of your attention. There's usually a difference in the amount of thought required when deciding on an ice cream flavor vs. a career choice. By considering the pros and cons and your own preferences regarding the options, you begin to see your choices more clearly. Also, consider the situation because some decisions can be reversed if necessary, so take this into consideration as you gain clarity about your decision.

If you aren't clear about what you want, it's difficult to move toward it. It is important to gain clarity to move forward. Being unable to make a decision can prevent you from making any movement at all. For example, if you can't decide whether to apply for an outside job or work from home, you may not take any action and end up doing neither. Instead, you spend five years thinking about it, discussing it with others, and suffering the consequences of inaction but never taking action.

Other times, you have to move to get clearer. You have to take that first step and see how you feel. Beginning to take action is a great way to gain clarity. Start with baby steps in the direction you think you want to go. If you are uncertain, test the waters and reevaluate as you slowly proceed.

Move in the direction you feel a bit better about and test it out, especially if you can adjust your direction as you gain more information and experience. If you decide to move in one direction then find out it was not as you had anticipated, you have more knowledge to continually refine your decision based on experience so you can get to the place that really makes you happy.

Understanding what you want and having the ability to explain in detail what you mean can help you understand your own hopes and needs better. Getting clear about what you want and focusing on the smaller details can help you understand what it is about your desire that makes you want to achieve it, and it also helps you get even more clarity. If you decide you want a new car, is it because you do not want to constantly worry about repairs or is it because you want to look nice as you drive around town in a fancy new car, or is it both?

On a piece of paper, make a list of the things you want in seven areas of your life. Include the areas of Career/Business, Finances/Money, Wellness/Appearance, Family/Fun Time, Relationships, Personal and any others you would like to write down. Start each sentence with "I want.". This exercise is meant to help you become a little bit clearer about your future. Keep your list handy because you will return to it again in the next chapter.

HOW LOOKING INSIDE HELPS YOUR CHILD

Helping your child figure out what makes them happy and inspired, as well as why they make excuses that may prevent them from reaching their goals, can greatly benefit them now and in the future. You can model and gently guide your child as you discuss these topics in age-appropriate ways. Remember to take your child's age and level of understanding into consideration. It may be as simple as clarifying with a very young child which choice they selected and why, having a dinner discussion and sharing your exercises or worksheets with a much older child, or anything in between.

Model and discuss taking responsibility.
Being positive and not making excuses will teach your child to do the same. When your child makes an excuse about why they are not doing something they should be doing or wanted to do, and places blame away from themselves, nicely ask them what other ways they could try to reach the results they want to achieve. Help them through the process of exploring the real reason why they aren't moving forward or reaching their desired goal. If you follow this process each time your child makes excuses, they will start thinking differently and will eventually begin to follow this process themselves. Explain the concept of taking 100 percent responsibility when your child is old enough to understand. This is a great skill to teach your child that many adults today have difficulty mastering. Getting rid of excuses will

help your child in school, future jobs and relationships. It will help your child feel more accomplished. Additionally, when your child observes you catching yourself when you start to make an excuse, it may help you figure out what is really holding you back, allowing you to successfully model and reinforce the importance of being 100 percent responsible.

Identify what makes your child happy.

Having a discussion with an older child about what makes them happy, or helping them become clear about what they want, can teach them more about themselves. Many people don't take the time to sit down and have this discussion. When your child says they are bored, instead of telling them to go find something to do, explore with them what kind of things make them happy, and soon it may be easier to not only help them find something to do but also inspire them.

Identifying what makes your child happy can often provide other alternatives to get the same desired results. For instance, a child may be really focused on the fact that they want to go to a friend's house, but it may not be possible at the time. In this example, when the parent delves further into the reason why the child really wants to go, the parent discovers there is another way to get a similar result that *is* possible. After discussing in more detail about why the child wants to go, the parent finds out that it is because they are excited to play with a friend's building kit. After asking a few questions about why they are so excited to do this, the mom discovers that her child is fascinated by how things work. This is something the parent would not have found out if the conversation ended at "no." This new information leads to a discussion about the child's fascination about what is inside objects that makes them work. Seeing the child light up while discussing the topic leads the mom to identify an activity that the child is very happy about substituting for their original request, addresses the reason they want to go to their friend's house in the first place, and may even further inspire the child's interest in technology.

I once had a similar conversation with my son. I offered my son a chance to get some tools and explore the inside of a broken, unplugged VCR, and he was happily busy for two hours. He removed all the wires and filled up a cup with screws and nuts, all the while fascinated by what he discovered, and I learned about something that lit up my son.

So, by asking questions and observing how your child talks about or focuses on things throughout their day, it can help both of you identify what makes them happy and inspired…and it may even mitigate a meltdown or two!

Another way to discover what makes your child happy is to share some of your own hopes and dreams with your child over dinner and invite your child to do the same. This can be a wonderful eye-opening discussion as well as a great bonding exercise, and you may find out something you never knew about your child. If your child is older, you may also want to discuss and share the *Happy Hunting Worksheet* with them so they can look for patterns within their own happiness.

Encourage your child to make simple decisions.
Children can develop the habit of saying, "I don't care," "I don't know," or "It doesn't matter" at a very early age. Habits are hard to break. When you hear your child say one of these phrases, ask your child to think for a minute, and if they could only pick one choice, ask them which one would make them happier. Discuss the options and explore their feelings about the choices. Explain that sometimes making decisions can be difficult so practicing with smaller decisions can help them in the future. This will help your child gain clarity, increase happiness and practice important decision-making skills.

LOOK INSIDE REVIEW

1. By taking full responsibility for your feelings and actions and not making excuses or blaming other people or circumstances, you can take control of your life!

2. Exploring what makes *you* happy by looking for patterns found throughout the happiest moments in your life and the happiest dreams for your future can help you discover themes that contribute to your happiness.

3. Being clear about what you want makes it easier to move toward your goals, so start practicing by making simple decisions every day.

Look Inside Exercises

1. Take 100 percent responsibility and complete the *I'm in Control Worksheet*. Make a list of excuses you use often that have stopped you from moving forward. Once the list is complete, go back and brainstorm the steps you could take to crush those excuses. Return to this sheet as needed until you come up with ways to crush all your excuses.

2. Complete the *Happy Hunting Worksheet*. After brainstorming or visualizing, make a list of the times you have been the happiest in your life. What were you doing? Where were you? Were you with someone or alone? After you complete the list, try to find the common themes that occur in the list. You may also use this same process to find common themes in your hopes and dreams for your ideal life.

3. Stop saying "I don't care," "I don't know," "It doesn't matter" or any similar phrases. Instead, take a minute, think about it, visualize it, focus on your internal feelings and respond with something like, "Seeing a movie would be great!"

4. On a sheet of paper, make a list of the things you want in all seven areas of your life, including Career/Business,

Finances/Money, Wellness/Appearance, Family/Fun Time, Relationships, Personal and any others you would like to include. Keep this paper to use in the next chapter.

5. Feel grateful that by looking inside, both you and your child will benefit.

Look Inside Exercises to Help Your Child

1. When your child makes an excuse, talk about ways to achieve what they didn't or don't think they can do and share some of your own experiences with your child, when appropriate. If you slip and make an excuse yourself, correct yourself and let your child help you determine why your excuse statement is not true. Discuss and share the *I'm in Control Worksheet* with an older child.

2. When your child makes a request that you have to say no to, dig deeper to discover what it is about the request that makes your child happy, and then suggest alternate ways to fulfill the request that might excite and inspire them. Discuss and share the *Happy Hunting Worksheet* with an older child.

3. When you hear your child use phrases like, "I don't care," "I don't know," or "It doesn't matter," help your child get clear. Ask your child what they really want. Discuss the options and explore their feelings about the choices.

4. Share some of your hopes and dreams with your child over dinner and invite your child to do the same.

I'M IN CONTROL WORKSHEET

Brainstorm and make a list of excuses you use often that have stopped you from moving forward. Fill out only the middle column and leave the last column empty for now.

Example	I can't start a photography business because I do not have the money to return to school.	I can learn online, join a Facebook photography group, find a mentor, read a photography book or practice with a friend. These are all ways I can learn more and take steps to get started.
Excuse #1		
Excuse #2		
Excuse #3		
Excuse #4		
Excuse #5		
Excuse #7		

Now, follow the example and brainstorm the steps you will take to CRUSH every one of your excuses. YOU are 100 percent responsible for your life!

HAPPY HUNTING WORKSHEET

Think about the times you were the happiest throughout your entire life. Think about childhood, recent events and future hopes and dreams. Answer the following 3 questions about each happy occurrence.

What were you doing?	Where were you?	Who were you with (alone, friends, relatives, partner)?

Now that you are done, find common themes
and include them in your life as often as you can.

CHAPTER 3

EXPLORE YOUR PASSIONS AND DESIRES

Do you know what makes you tick? What really gets you excited? What do you feel passionate about? You may already know the answers to these questions, or you may still be searching. This chapter will help you explore your passions and show you an easy way to create goals related to your passions and interests. Passions are often broad. Achievable goals are usually much more defined. For example, your passion may be to help others, but there are so many ways that you can do that. You can have a goal to become a therapist, volunteer at a school, provide advice to friends, help your neighbor in the garden or become a cancer research scientist. Those examples are just a few of the hundreds of ways you can fulfill that passion. Exploring your passion and desires will help you discover ways to get excited, motivated and live life to the fullest.

Learn how passions and goals relate to each other.
Passions can develop or change over time, but in general, a passion is a strong affection or enthusiasm for something. It is true that anything you truly enjoy and are enthusiastically interested in could be one of your passions. It is also true that just because you are passionate about something, does not always mean you will easily be able to achieve any goal related to that passion. If you loved horses and decided you wanted to write a book about horses, but you soon discovered that you did not like writing at all, it might be best to either find another way to enjoy your passion for horses or find someone to help you write the book so you could achieve that goal. One example of

getting help reaching that goal could be to record the book and then use a transcriber and editor to prepare the book for publishing. It is important to align your passion and your goals, but it is also important to create goals you enjoy achieving. Even though one of my passions is to help people, I did not have to become a nurse or clergy member to do this because there are so many other ways to live my passion. As you begin to read about passions, please do not stress if you cannot identify one glaring passion in your life, because some people can, and other people may discover they have several more subtle passions.

While it is not always possible to achieve every goal related to your passions, creating goals that are related to your passion can be helpful in keeping you on course. You may be more likely to reach a goal that is related to your passion because you may be more motivated to achieve the goal, and you may enjoy the process more. If you do not enjoy the process you are taking to reach your goals, you may want to reevaluate your goal or redesign it. There are other times, such as when trying to lose weight, when you may not necessarily enjoy the process, but you can focus on the outcome such as the weight loss and the positive habits you will develop by completing the process. That alone may be enough to motivate you to successfully achieve the goal. As you can now see, having a goal related to something you are passionate about can be helpful, but it is not always necessary.

Examine your passions.
The *What Makes Me Tick Worksheet* at the end of the chapter takes you through a simple process to discover your interests or passions. Here are the questions you will need to think about as you complete it.

What are four positive qualities or characteristics people have said about you that you believe are true? Maybe over the years, friends or co-workers have complimented you about or mentioned how you have a knack for doing something. It doesn't have to be a specific task like decorating a room in your house; it could even be general comments about your creativity.

The next question to consider is, which of the four qualities do you really relate to and feel describe you the best? Be truthful with yourself when you answer this question and do not allow your limiting beliefs or what you think you should or shouldn't be like affect your answer. Creative, reliable, caring, knowledgeable, great with children, and kind are just a few examples of the infinite number of qualities you can choose.

The next question is what are you doing that helps others to see those qualities and characteristics? Do you decorate your house for holidays, give friends advice or post information on your Internet pages?

Lastly, imagine you are elderly and happily looking back at your life. What matters the most to you? Why are you so happy and satisfied with your life? What did you do during your life to make you feel that way?

Using the worksheet instructions and your answers, complete the blanks at the bottom of the worksheet with your answers to come up with a life passion sentence that you feel really describes you.

Discover your desires.
Now that you have a better idea of what you are passionate about, let's look further and find out what really makes you happy. Let me ask you a question? What would make you happy? I don't mean things like having a bowl of ice cream at the end of a difficult day. I mean *really* happy. If you could have your ideal life, what would it be like?

Remember when you used to sit in class, and before you knew it, your mind went elsewhere? Well, it's time to do that again and this time, you won't get in trouble if you get caught doing it! Take some time and daydream. What would your ideal life be like? Where would you live? Who would you be with? What type of place would you live in? How would you dress? What would you accomplish? Where would you hang out? How would you get around? Don't worry about how you will achieve this or if you feel it's realistic or not. We will get to that later. For now, grab something warm to drink, relax, get comfy and have fun visualizing your ideal life.

After you have visualized what would really make you happy for a while, it's time to take the list of wants from all areas of your life that you created after reading the last chapter, revise it as needed and start to fill in the *Clarity on Steroids Worksheet* at the end of this chapter. Transfer each of your wants from the list onto the worksheet. Start each sentence with "I want," but unlike the last chapter's exercise, this time, make it as long and as detailed as you can. Really dream. See the colors. Smell the smells. Hear the noises. Get very clear. Go from the bird's eye view to the microscopic view. Be very specific. For instance, instead of saying, "I want to lose weight," say "I want to weigh 145 lbs. by my next birthday." Write each desire so anyone could take out that worksheet at a date in the future and determine if you achieved each goal. The more descriptive you make it, the more likely you will get to your true desires and the more accountable you will be. Do this for all the areas of your life that are included on the *Clarity on Steroids Worksheet*. If there is anything you did not place on the original list you created in the last chapter, include that on the worksheet too.

Describe each desire in great detail. If you want a house, write down every detail of that house. What color is it? Is there a garage? How many bedrooms are there? What colors are the walls? Are the floors carpeted, tiled or wood? The clearer you are, the better it will be. Now, go back and read over your list and make sure you did not only include the things you think you can make happen, but also everything you want, whether you think it is possible or not. Make sure you have included things that stretch you. If not, add them now. Have fun with this exercise and in a little bit, I'll share what happened to me the first time I did this exercise.

Review your desires frequently.
That was fun, but now what do you do with your list of desires? It is important that you look at your desires several times a day. Some people write them on a note card or paper and put the detailed list of desires by their bed to read first thing in the morning and right before bed. Other people like to carry the list

on a card in their purse or pocket. Some people are more visual and like to create a collage they can look at every day, and others include a picture or words on their computer/phone background or screensaver. Some people place a sticky note containing the list on their bathroom mirror or in the kitchen so they see it every morning when they get up. Whatever method or methods you choose should ensure your detailed desires are somewhere you will see them often. The more often you review the list, the more you will be reminded about your hopes and desires.

Feel the excitement.
It is important to make sure that when you look at your list, you feel the excitement and emotion of how you will actually feel when you receive the items on your list.

For example, if one of the items on your list was to complete a marathon, imagine yourself crossing the finish line, crowds clapping and yelling, sweat dripping off you as your feet hit the hard pavement, your loved ones watching proudly and cheering and the feeling of accomplishment and pride you feel within. You may even want to use this practice as a way to get motivated before heading out the door for a run. Do this with each item on the list. Take a minute to imagine that you just made each dream come true and feel the intense emotions inside of you. This will create the excitement and light the fire within you to bring you even closer to your dreams.

Embrace your goals.
Going forward, we are now going to refer to your *Clarity on Steroids Worksheet* list as your "goals" because if you really want to achieve what is on your list, it is time to learn the simple process to begin the steps to get there. The first time I listed my goals in detail, I really had fun with it. I plotted out my goals in all the areas with great detail and various time lines. I made short-term and long-term goals. I was happy and not really trying to improve in some of the areas of my life, but I filled up my sheet of paper and gave it very serious thought. I read my goals often.

As will happen in time, my goals continued to evolve and as I refined them, I was no longer using that particular list because I created an updated list. One day, several years later while on a mastermind call, which is a group call where participants provide feedback and accountability to other members, I made the decision to look at my original goals and see how I did. As I reviewed them with my husband before the next mastermind call, we were both a bit freaked out by how closely they resembled our current life. One goal was my desire for a corner unit condo with a tile floor, cool lighting, on the fourth or fifth floor, with a balcony, floor-to-ceiling windows, and overlooking the water. I wanted it to have shops, restaurants, entertainment, cafes and a grocery store all within walking distance. This goal actually originated as my dream for a beach home.

Well, about 3 years after creating the original goal, my husband and I temporarily relocated, and guess what? We were living in a condo with every single one of those features even though I had totally forgotten about the details of this goal! As we reread the description of each feature, while sitting in our condo, the feelings that we both experienced were unbelievable. Experiencing the strangest feeling in my stomach, I felt a bit relieved when I read the last feature aloud. I said, "Well there is one difference. We aren't overlooking the ocean." My husband asked me to read the exact words for that feature again. I then read out loud, "overlooking the water." He replied, "The fact that our balcony directly overlooks an Olympic-size pool doesn't count?" So be super clear when you list every detail and complete this exercise! We laughed, I refined the goal and we are now preparing for that beachfront condo!

To this day, we still marvel at the success of all the goals on that page. When I first wrote my detailed goals, I wanted to believe, but I never imagined I would have achieved almost all the goals. The more I reviewed them and the clearer each detail became, the more positive I felt that I could reach them. You can have the same success, because being crystal clear and setting specific time frames helps you determine what it is you really want. Learning the simple steps included in the rest of this book will help catapult you directly toward your dreams.

One person who used this process to examine her passion and set an important goal in her life was Alana. She loved dance. She had been dancing since before she was three years of age. She was attending college in Philadelphia with a promising artist scholarship for dance when she decided to change majors to a career that she felt was a bit more stable financially and would not require her to move to different areas of the country for a job.

After thinking it over, she decided she wanted to become an English teacher because she also loved literature and working with children. She changed colleges and majors and began working toward her degree to teach English literature. She continued dancing in her spare time and during the last semester before graduating with an education degree, she started to have conflicting feelings about her future goals. She knew any changes she made at that time would require a very major decision, and she wanted to be certain about what she really wanted for her future.

After much thought and discussion, she went through the process of identifying her passions. This process helped her discover that although she loved literature, dance was really where her heart was. Once she was certain that this was the direction she wanted to take, she decided teaching dance would allow her to pursue her passion regarding dance and allow her to work with and mentor children of all ages. She discovered these were both important considerations when making her decision. Her desire to become a dance studio owner required a big change in plans, but once she acknowledged her passions and set her goal to become a dance studio owner, she was on her way.

Acknowledging her passion and setting her goal were two very important steps that were necessary for her to feel comfortable with her decision and confidently take the next steps to move forward. From there, she continued the process that is discussed in greater detail throughout this book, which included brainstorming multiple possibilities, breaking down her goals and starting to take the steps necessary to reach her goal, even in the face of fear. She had to maneuver around many obstacles such as changing her major at a late date, locating and affording a dance studio, locating enough students to cover her expenses, business planning and paying the bills for her business and her personal life. Although this was quite a big task for a 21-year-old, the process of gaining clarity about her desires, defining her passions and setting a very clear goal was instrumental in her eventual success in reaching her very large goal.

Creating goals from your own desires is an important step in the process of designing your ideal future. You will learn easy ways to make your large goals much more manageable in chapter five. You will even learn how to organize your time so you can work toward your goals during your already busy day in chapter seven, so keep reading! You have started the process by exploring your passions and creating detailed goals in all areas of your life. You are on your way!

HOW EXPLORING PASSIONS AND DESIRES HELPS YOUR CHILD

Introduce goals to your child.

Your child has passions and desires, just as you do. When you understand the types of things and activities your child enjoys as well as your child's desires, it is much easier to support them and understand their actions. As your child grows, your child will observe you and see the importance of having goals and working toward them to reach the desired outcome. You can introduce the concept of desires becoming goals to your child in an age appropriate manner at a very young age. This may also help at times when your child is impatient and wants that toy now. This depends of course on may factors such as temperament, tiredness, and the cognitive ability to understand the concept you are explaining. Let me explain how.

For an older child, you can explain you would like your outcomes right now too, but that is not realistic You can explain that you know you *will* get what you want eventually by working toward your goal step by step, and they can do the same thing. As a parent, you can help your child think through this process. If your six-year-old comes up to you and says they want a certain toy, and if it is reasonable for you to purchase it, ask them if they have money to buy it. You can tell them that if they don't have money now, there are ways to get the toy a bit later by making something called a "goal." Explain that a goal is like playing a board game. You take steps and do the things that will let you move closer to what you want, and then you finally get it.

Another analogy that can be explained to children with the ability to understand, is the way we walk up the steps one by one to get to the top. You could suggest, for example, that every day they pick up their room, they can earn X cents or X points, and each time they do that, it is like going up one more step. When they get X amount, they will reach their goal (the top of the steps) and be able to get the toy or the trip to the playground they wanted. You can make it a fun game by using an old board game with the spaces labeled with a marker or covered with taped pieces of paper. You could also write out a chart, place checkmarks on a calendar or use any other age-appropriate way your child can understand. Remember to keep using the word *goal* so your child will understand the concept. It may also help to tell your child about a simple goal you are working toward so you can work on your goals together and share your progress.

This technique can be introduced in a much simpler way for younger children. For example, if your child wants to go to the ice cream store, draw 5 ice cream cones on a paper so they can visualize it. Tell your child that every day they go to bed on time and stay in bed, the next morning when they wake up, together you will cross off one ice cream cone, and when they are all crossed off, you will celebrate by getting ice cream at the ice cream store.

The secret is to introduce the word *goal* once your child is old enough to understand. Make sure your child understands some type of action is required to reach the goal, and then make a very big deal when the goal is achieved. Congratulate your child for following each small step and for not giving up. Even though the goal examples included paid items, this concept can be used for a play date, craft time, or any no-cost option.

Understanding goals may also help when a child is impatient or really wants a toy, as mentioned earlier. Of course, the wrong time to try this is when your child is tired or in the middle of a tantrum, so please use your parental wisdom regarding the ideal time to introduce this concept. It is best to introduce this when your child mentions their desire for something, after seeing it on television or seeing a friend with a toy, and not in the heat of the moment while shopping!

If you child is older and is having trouble reaching a goal and wants to give up, show them how to create smaller sub goals to get to the larger goal. For instance, I will earn X amount per week for 4 weeks instead of setting the goal too high with only one large dollar amount. The smaller goals are more achievable, require less patience and will help your child stay on track. We will discuss the topic of helping your child learn to break down goals in greater detail in chapter five.

Also, it is important for your child to learn that if the desired outcome has changed, a goal can be revised. In the example above, your child may decide they now would rather have the cool new scooter that just came out instead of the originally desired item. Let your child know it can be ok to change a goal if it is no longer desired. Help them evaluate why they are changing the goal, the impact it may have on them or others and what changes they need to make. Explore how much money has been saved so far for the old item, the price of the scooter they now want and what steps they will now need to take to reach their new goal. This can be modified for any age, just make sure your child understands the concept in their own words. Older children can even keep track of the math and may come up with their own unique ideas about how to reach the goal. Share the goals you think are appropriate for your child's age and let your child see that parents and many others have goals they also work towards.

If your child is older, it may be fun to work on creating goals together. Select one you will work on and have your child do the same. Being accountable to each other by sharing the detailed sub goal you are working on and discussing if you met your goal at the end of each week will help both of you. This process will help you determine what your child deems important. It is an opportunity to discuss revising, refining and the appropriateness of goals. When working on goals together, it's important to follow through with your own goal, because you are the model for your child.

Play the Goal To Whole game.
Just about everything that was ever created and made whole by man was first a thought, which then became a many-step goal, before it was created. One way to teach this message is to play a game called Goal To Whole. In this game, each player takes turns naming items around the house and the other player has to try to list each small goal or step that had to be achieved before the final item was complete or whole.

An example for a younger child might be a dresser. First, someone decided they needed a place for their clothes. Then someone had to get wood and nails and then someone had to build a dresser.

The same example for an older child might include, someone needed a place to store their clothes, a tree had to grow, a tree had to be cut down, the wood had to be put on a truck, the pieces had to be cut out of the wood, the cut pieces had to be nailed or glued together and painted or stained, the dresser had to be taken to the store, the customer had to come buy the dresser and the dresser had to be taken to the house and then it had to be placed in the bedroom.

This game can be fun for any age and lead to learning opportunities when an older child gets stumped or players disagree and the information has to be researched on the Internet or by asking a knowledgeable adult. You can play for fun without keeping a score, or older children and adults can keep score in many creative ways, but for most ages, being able to reasonably explain the general process would count as one point. Not only does this game create fun, but it also reminds the players that many common household items we may take for granted each day often require a lengthy process before they arrive at our house. Gratitude can be reinforced at this time also.

To wrap up the conversation about goals, just remember to introduce the concept of goals to your child at a level they can understand, and expand it as they grow, to ensure they can fully understand the concept you are teaching them…and don't forget to celebrate the large achievements!

EXPLORE YOUR PASSIONS AND DESIRES REVIEW

1. A passion is a strong affection or enthusiasm for something.
2. Determining what you are passionate about can make it easier for you to create goals you will be motivated to achieve.
3. Daydreaming is fun and it is a good way to start to clarify your desires.
4. Being as clear and detailed as possible when thinking about desires will help you as you turn them into goals.
5. Selecting specific time frames for your goals can help you stay accountable.
6. Reviewing your desires frequently will ensure that you remain focused on them, even on the busiest of days.
7. Reviewing and visualizing your goals will help you stay focused on and feel excited about your goals.

Explore Your Passions and Desires Exercises

1. Complete the *What Makes Me Tick Worksheet* at the end of this chapter to gain a better understanding of your passions.
2. Get comfortable and daydream about your ideal life, using all your senses. Do not make excuses or limit your imagination while doing this step.
3. Fill out the *Clarity on Steroids Worksheet* at the end of this chapter. Write down your dreams and don't forget to be detailed, include time frames and explore all areas of your life.
4. Create a way to look at your goals every day by reviewing the *Clarity on Steroids Worksheet*, making a collage, hanging a list near your mirror, writing the list on a card,

putting the goals on your phone/computer, or any way that works for you.

5. Read your goals at least twice a day while visualizing and feeling the excitement of achieving them.

6. Feel grateful that by focusing on your goals, both you and your child will benefit.

Explore Your Passions and Desires Exercises to Help Your Child

1. Model how you work toward and achieve your own goals.

2. Introduce the concept of goals to your child in an age-appropriate manner using some of the examples in the chapter. Don't forget to celebrate the achievements.

3. Help your child create and work toward their own goals and expand their understanding as they get older, by including such concepts as sub goals, revising goals, evaluating goals, and playing the Goal To Whole game.

WHAT MAKES ME TICK WORKSHEET

List 4 qualities/characteristics that people have said about you, that you believe are true.

Select two of the qualities from above that you relate to and feel describe you the best.

What are two things you enjoy doing that helps others to see the above listed qualities?

If you were elderly and happily looking back at your life, what would matter the most to you? Why are you so happy and satisfied with your life? What did you do during your life to make you feel that way?

Using your answers to the last three questions above, create your life passion sentence.

Example: My passion is to use <u>my uniqueness and creativity</u> to <u>teach and inspire others</u> to <u>unleash their own happiness and ability to create.</u>

CLARITY ON STEROIDS WORKSHEET

Copy your "I want" statements from the list of wants you created in the last chapter, as well as any new desires you have thought of since creating the first list. Next, read each statement. Close your eyes. Visualize it, hold it, smell it and feel the excitement, as if you just reached your desire! Do this for one minute or more, and then document every detail about your desire, including when you will receive it, in the last column of the worksheet.

EXAMPLE Personal	I want a new car.	I want a new 4 door black and chrome Audi A4 with beige leather seats and a sunroof. I want less than 25 thousand miles on the car when I purchase it by my birthday.
Career/Business	I want	
Finances/Money	I want	
Wellness/Appearance	I want	
Family time/Fun time	I want	
Relationships	I want	
Personal	I want	
Others	I want	

CHAPTER 4

BELIEVE IN YOURSELF

Ok, now you may be thinking, I've been practicing being more positive and it's really helping. I explored what makes me happy and I have my detailed list of all the things that I want in my life, but now what do I do? How will I ever achieve my dreams?

Well, let me explain a bit more about positivity. Positivity includes everything discussed in chapter one, but there is another aspect of positivity we haven't discussed, and that includes positivity about one's self. This is a very important topic and is necessary to understand the concept of positivity entirely. Positive thinking in general is one topic, and an important one at that, but thinking positively about your own ability to succeed is crucial, because if you do not think you can succeed, you will severely limit or block your ability to do so. There will be times when your brain will start pulling up past experiences or conversations called negative self-talk. You may be thinking, "I don't have the money," or "I don't have the right expertise/education," or "I wouldn't know where to begin." I used to think the same things, so let me tell you how to get over this hurdle and think positively about your own ability to reach your goals and achieve your desires.

Replace negative thoughts with positive thoughts.
The first thing you have to do is replace the negative thoughts that you have about yourself with positive thoughts. Every thought you think reinforces your beliefs. There is even research that has found that your thoughts can actually change your brain chemistry. Each time you have a negative thought, stop, rephrase it in a positive way, smile, and move on. It will take practice, but

you must change your beliefs to move forward. For example, if you catch yourself thinking, "I'll never be able to run in a marathon," change this thought to a more positive thought. You could change it to, "If I continue to consistently practice and build up my endurance, I will be able to complete a marathon."

Replace negative words with positive words.
Another way to stay more positive is by getting rid of negative words like "can't," "don't," "have to," and "must." Just stop using them. If you find you do use a negative term, stop and ask yourself, "What do I want?" or "What can I do?" For example, if you say, "I don't want to work all day and never see my kids," think about the outcome you want. Instead of focusing on what you don't want to do, replace the word "don't" with what you *do* want. You could say, "I want a job where I can work and spend plenty of quality time with my children." It may not be easy the first time, but you can really do just about anything you want to do, once you learn to stop limiting yourself. By rephrasing your thought, you identify a goal. When you identify a goal, you become much clearer, and having a clear goal is one of the first steps required before you start to take action and achieve that goal.

Believe it's possible.
Believing in yourself and not limiting yourself and your beliefs leads to success. Did you know that a person who was blind, successfully climbed a dangerous mountain? A farmer ran his first ever multiday marathon race and set the record by 12 hours, and many people from all backgrounds have gone from making no money to making millions. Why were those people able to do things that others, more experienced or more knowledgeable, could not? It was because they *believed* they could, so they took action, worked hard, did not give up and achieved their goals. If they did not believe they had a chance of reaching their goals, they may have dismissed their initial thoughts by telling themselves that they had no chance of succeeding and they would have never achieved their goals.

One day, I was working with a young mother who was addicted to opiates. She tried everything to get off them. She went to clinics, hospitals and stayed at rehab facilities but couldn't stop. One day she called and she said she was ready to stop, and she knew she would be successful. She spoke confidently. I asked her why she felt more certain this time, and she said that her boyfriend always told her she would never be able to quit taking such an addicting drug and she believed him. She said she finally realized he didn't want her to stop because he knew she would leave him if she were able to quit. She said once she stopped believing what her partner said to her and started to believe in herself, she knew she could stop. She had a big job ahead of her, but with her belief in herself and the support of others, she was doing well and remained drug-free for more than a year after she called me.

Your success can start with a single thought. You must start to believe in yourself right now. If the farmer, the blind climber, the new millionaires and the drug-addicted mother could do it, so can you!

Learn how beliefs can be limiting.
People limit themselves every day without even knowing it! Where do they develop these limiting beliefs? It could be that in the past, they had an experience and someone told them they couldn't do something. It could have been a teacher in school, a parent, a kid down the street, or several past experiences. Have you ever been told, "Money doesn't grow on trees," "You only think about yourself," "Act your age" or any of the hundreds of other statements people repeat without giving much thought to the meaning? Often, the sayings are not meant to harm, but they are just sayings or beliefs people have been repeating, without much thought for years and years.

Kate had always dreamed of working in the marketing division of a Fortune 500 company. Because her family did not have the resources for room and board, she attended a local community college and lived at home. After graduating, she said she transferred to a state college because the tuition was lower than the private schools that she researched. When she graduated, she began looking for jobs in her local area even though she always talked about how she would love to work for a large corporation. One day, we were talking and I asked her which corporations she would like to work for. She listed several companies but always ended by saying "But I'd never get hired there," or something similar. When I asked her why she thought they would not hire her, she responded, "The big corporations only want to hire people with degrees from prestigious colleges and not someone from a community college or a state school." I asked her if she thought she could do the work that was required in the type of position she described, and she immediately answered yes. I then told her about someone I knew who attended community college and was successfully working at a Fortune 500 corporation. I also explained to her that NASA's first female shuttle commander, Eileen Collins, attended the very same community college she did, and many people have had great success after attending community colleges and state schools. As I said this, her eyes widened. Kate's limiting belief that she would never get her dream job because she did not attend what she considered a "prestigious" college was holding her back from achieving her dreams. Once she let go of that belief, she was on her way to the job of her dreams. It has been a few years since that conversation and Kate is now working in the marketing division of one of the Fortune 500 Companies she mentioned that day!

Replace your limiting beliefs.
It is very likely that you may be limiting yourself without even knowing it. Sometimes, people use limiting beliefs as a way to feel better about themselves by blaming their circumstances on things that are out of their control.

For this next exercise, you will use the *Beliefs That Halt My Success Worksheet* at the end of the chapter. First, read over the goals you wrote on your *Clarity on Steroids Worksheet* from chapter three and make a list of the beliefs that pop into you head as you read them. If you didn't even write some of the goals down earlier, because you discounted them before you even put pen to paper, include those too. Also, include any general beliefs you have, such as, "Only people with good paying jobs can save money," or "I can't lose weight because of my genetics," or "No one cares what I think." Sometimes, if you complete this exercise with a friend or a family member, they may be able to point out things you may not even see yourself. As you get into this exercise, you may even find that you actually start giggling at how silly some of the beliefs you hold really are.

After reading the two examples below, follow the outline and fill out the worksheet starting with your belief. Be honest with yourself as you do this exercise. It's time to discover that your beliefs are really just perceptions you believe to be true. You may also be unconsciously using the beliefs as an excuse for why you have not moved forward.

This exercise can be eye opening. You may find that you limit yourself because you believe you have no power to change your situation, but after looking deeper, you will find that your belief is just that—only a belief. Once you work through the limiting belief, the sky is the limit and you will become the only person who determines your happiness and future success.

Here is example belief #1: I need to devote all my time to my family because I have a new baby.

Ways that it limits me: It limits me because I spend all my time doing things for others and doing nothing for myself. Because of this, I am tired, stressed and unhappy at times.

How I want it to be: I love my baby and family, but I want to have some time to take care of myself and do things I enjoy. Doing so would help me feel happier and decrease my stress.

New belief: It is important and healthy for me to devote time to me, as well as to my family.

Here is example belief #2: I can't have a fulfilling career because I don't have a college degree.

Ways that it limits me: It limits me because I don't consider applying for many types of jobs because I think the companies will never hire me. Instead, I only apply for lower-level jobs that don't pay well.

How I want it to be: I want to have a job that I enjoy and am proud of. I want to be able to pay my bills and show others I can be successful.

New belief: There are many fulfilling jobs that do not require a college degree, which will help me develop new skills and pay my bills. I will start applying to many different types of jobs that interest me, so I can get more experience and find a job I will be proud of.

Try following the same pattern for each of your statements and then highlight the new beliefs you created so you can review them when necessary. Now, sit up tall and slowly and confidently read each new positive belief out loud while you feel the power it provides. Feel the shift that is beginning to take place as you realize that one of the things that limits you is the obstacle your thoughts provide. Limiting beliefs limit your ability to consider all possibilities and greatly decrease your chance of success. They stop you from moving forward and quash your dreams in an instant. Get those thoughts out of your head and replace them with your new positive beliefs.

 Don't get me wrong, I'm not saying everything will be super easy. After all, you may have been unconsciously thinking those thoughts for most of your life, but if a blind person can climb a dangerous mountain, you can replace your negative thoughts with the potential you really possess to reach your goals. You will feel better and your confidence will begin to soar. You can do this. I know you can because you want to move forward, so give it a try. I have faith in you!

Don't compare yourself to others.
Avoid falling into the habit of comparing yourself to someone else. No two people are exactly alike. Comparisons don't help you because you may never know the full story of someone else's life. If you had a friend who was in a leadership position at her

company and you thought, "Wow she is doing so much better than me," would that really be true? Think about it. This is your perception. Just because you perceive her to have a job that you feel is a "good" job, does not mean she is better or smarter.

When we compare ourselves to others, we usually only compare one aspect. But if we look at all aspects of a person's life, we see that everyone has strengths and weaknesses, just like your friend and yourself. Your friend may excel in her leadership position, but she may not be as empathetic or as talented at music as you are. So, just don't compare.

Now, let's go back to the earlier example of your friend who was a leader at her company. If you really valued being a leader at a company, couldn't you do what you needed to do to get there? Yes you could! I'm not saying you would want to, or that you should, but if you wanted to, you could research and study about leadership, get leadership training if needed, network with others, or whatever you needed to do to apply and get a similar job, just like she did. It may take time or not, but if you made it your top priority and didn't make excuses, you could find a way to get there. So, she is not any better than you. She just did something you have not yet done but could do if you wanted to! So, the next time you catch yourself comparing yourself to someone else, remind yourself that you have many strengths too and there's no one else on this earth quite like you!

Celebrate your past successes.

Another way to remind yourself of your ability to succeed, is to think about all your past successes. Now, before you say you can't think of any, let me tell you why this is important. Your brain makes it easier for you to remember strong emotions. Because of this, that time you were totally embarrassed in front of the whole class, or the time you were really devastated when you weren't selected for the team, will naturally stand out in your mind. You need to bring your successes forward to crowd out the other feelings and memories, so you can move forward confidently. Use the *Victory List Worksheet* at the end of this chapter and make a list of all the successful things that happened to you starting as far back as you can remember. I call it the "Me Museum." Did you draw a picture that the teacher hung up in elementary school? Did you do well on a test? Did you win a race or help a neighbor? Did you try out and get selected for a team? The thoughts will come slowly at first, but soon, you will think of more and more. After you compose your list, think of the largest accomplishment that comes to mind and visualize it to relive it. Feel the emotions as if you were there. Feel how powerful it makes you feel. Remember the sounds, the smells, and the excitement. Close your eyes and recall every detail.

As you continue the steps in this book, if you start to doubt yourself or hear any of that negative self-talk, return to your Me Museum, read over your list, and feel the emotion you felt at the time, which will help build up your confidence and get back on track. Many successful people use this tip before attending important meetings or speaking to build up their confidence. Some people put symbols or photos that remind them of past successes around their office to achieve the same effect. Others relive that great moment right before they enter an important meeting or negotiation.

Don't forget to document the new successes you achieve as you move through the steps in this book. Document them on your computer, phone or notebook and add them to your Me Museum. Were you more positive today? Did you get rid of some of your limiting beliefs? Did you recall times when you did succeed? As you take more and more steps forward, you will gain even more confidence. Don't forget to celebrate your accomplishments, no matter how small, because that means you are moving forward, and moving forward builds confidence. Start that ball rolling right now!

HOW BELIEVING IN YOURSELF HELPS YOUR CHILD

Believing in yourself will also create a calmness and direction within you that will be positive for your child. When you are calmer and more content with your own life, and when you can envision a positive future for you and your child, you will be happier and your child will be able to sense that. That will create a calming environment for your child too, especially as an infant. When your baby can count on you and trust you to meet basic needs for love, food, affection and stimulation, attachment gets stronger. This causes your child to trust you. As a baby develops trust, it also helps them to feel safe and secure and handle stress better. Trust-building is a very important stage of development for babies as well as older children, and it impacts future relationship building.

Parents play an important role in their child's life. Children look to their parents for security as well as how to act, learn and believe. When you exhibit more confidence, you have less self-doubt, greater energy and motivation and you are able to handle a wide range of situations. This greatly impacts not only your life but also the life of your child.

When you stop saying things like "I can't" and "I'll never be able to," your child will not learn this destructive habit from you. If your child is a bit older and has already heard these statements and you hear your child make a similar statement, it is time to explain that you have stopped saying them because you found that they are not true and they keep you from doing great things.

Help your child replace negative words with positive ones.
When you notice your child using negative words like "I can't," "I don't," point it out to your child and explain how you are trying to use more positive words by changing the way you say the sentence. Show your child how to rephrase the sentence by replacing the negative word with a positive one. Instead of saying, "I don't want," ask them to say, "I want" and state what they *do* want instead. Explain that stating it that way will help them focus on a solution and the things they *can do* instead of on the problem.

Tell them that negative or complaining statements make us believe we can't do things we really can. Then, explain why the first statement your child made is not accurate. This will educate your child and increase your child's confidence. Ask your child to stop you if they hear you make a statement using a negative word and tell them you will do the same. At first, you may need to explain in a bit of detail about why the statement that was made was not true, but as you continue to do this, your child will catch on and eventually notice when they make negative statements.

You could go even further and agree that after either of you catch the other using a negative phrase, the person who hears the comment will explain to the person who made the comment why it is not true. I call this the "Catch and Return" game. It is always nice to hear positive feedback. Sometimes, your child will point out positive traits you possess that you never even thought about, and you can do the same for them. For an older child, you could even make a game out of it. For example, the person who is caught making the most negative statement excuses in a week will do one previously agreed upon chore for the other person at the end of the week.

Share why it's not a good idea to compare.
If you hear your child comparing their life or circumstances with others, explain to them that everyone has different strengths and weaknesses and that is what makes everyone unique. Explain why it is not a good idea to compare yourself to others, and provide examples related to your child's age and understanding. You can even use your child's favorite cartoon or movie characters to begin this discussion with a younger child. For example, If the television character Ernie is sad because he is not tall like Big Bird and cannot reach high items or see when people are in front of him at the movie theater, help your child explore Ernie's unique talents such as singing, playing musical instruments and his good sense of humor, even though he isn't tall, while also explaining that everyone is special in their own way.

For an older child who may be unfairly comparing themselves to someone else, use the same technique of pointing out that everyone has differing abilities in all areas, and point out several of their special abilities. With an older child, it is also important to explore your child's feelings as you discuss this with them to understand why your child is feeling this way and to identify if there are any underlying issues that may need to be discussed with your physician or other professionals, such as depression or anxiety.

Help your child feel more confident.
When you catch your child feeling like they cannot achieve a goal or are worried about passing a test or speaking in front of the class, remind your child about situations in the past when they were successful. Once you start doing this, they may be able to point out other instances they remember from school or other times when you may not have been present. It may be fun for them to draw pictures of some of the times they were able to do something they were worried about or excelled at something. They could even cut out pictures from magazines or print pictures from the computer to create a collage of all those times, and hang it in their bedroom or on the refrigerator as a reminder. This can also lead to a conversation about how to help them figure out what would make them feel more confident in their current situation. It may involve planning some practice time, talking about how they handled a similar fear in the past, talking positively about the outcome they hope to obtain, or all the above.

Help build your child's self-esteem.
Although there are many ways to help children build self-esteem, one simple way that I will discuss is to use labeled praise instead of general praise whenever possible. Labeled praise explains what a child is being praised for, such as, "I liked how you were respectful and used your quiet voice in the library," or "I was proud when you hugged your friend when she was crying," whereas general praise would be saying things such as "great job" or "you were good today." Use labeled praise when possible because general praise will show approval but will not tell your child what behaviors you liked.

Believe in yourself and model your own self-confidence to your child. Try the tips provided in this section, taking your child's age into consideration. Increased confidence and self-esteem will benefit your child in school, in social situations, and throughout life.

BELIEVE IN YOURSELF REVIEW

1. Your thoughts reinforce your beliefs. Negative thoughts reinforce negative beliefs and positive thoughts reinforce positive beliefs.

2. When you stop using negative statements and words, and instead ask yourself, "What *do* I want?" your desires become clearer.

3. Believing leads to doing. According to research, shifting your feelings can change your brain chemistry.

4. People who compare themselves to others often look at only one or two aspects of a person's life, not all areas. Everyone has strengths in different areas.

5. Recalling both past successes and emotionally reliving a large accomplishment has been shown to increase confidence.

Believe in Yourself Exercises

1. Stop using negative words such as *can't*, *won't*, and *don't*. Instead, say what you can do, will do or what you do want.

2. Change your beliefs. When you catch yourself saying a negative term, stop, think and rephrase the sentence to include the real reason, not the easy excuse. For example, instead of saying, "I don't do well in school," say, "I do well in school when I am learning something I am interested in and when I prepare for all homework and tests."

3. Use the *Beliefs That Halt My Success Worksheet* to make a list of all your limiting beliefs. Rewrite them in a positive way, and read them out loud. Do this exercise with a friend to have an even greater effect and possibly a few laughs if you uncover some silly beliefs!

4. Do not compare yourself to others. Everyone has different strengths.

5. Complete the *Victory List Worksheet*. Do not think about how big or small the victories were; instead, think about how great you felt when each happened. Review it periodically, especially when you need a boost in confidence.

6. Feel grateful that by increasing your confidence, both you and your child will benefit.

Believe in Yourself Exercises to Help Your Child

1. When you notice your child using negative words like "I can't" and "I don't," point it out to your child and help them rephrase the sentence in a positive way. For example, ask, "What do you want?"

2. If your child is older and able to understand, play the "Catch and Return Game." The player who catches the most negative or limiting comments made by the other player, while also explaining why they are not true, wins. For example, the person who is caught making the most negative statements/excuses in a week will do one previously agreed-upon chore for the other person at the end of the week.

3. If you hear your child comparing their life or their circumstances with others, explain to them that everyone has different strengths and weaknesses and that is what makes them unique.

4. Help your child practice something they want to improve, remind and encourage them to talk about how a current fear or worry was handled successfully by them in the past, and encourage them to talk positively about an outcome they hope to obtain. All this can help increase their confidence.

5. Use labeled praise with your child instead of general praise when possible because general praise will show approval, but it will not tell your child what behaviors you liked.

BELIEFS THAT HALT MY SUCCESS WORKSHEET

Everyone has beliefs that are inaccurate, yet we never even question them. Please follow the example and list each of your inaccurate beliefs, then document why each belief is stopping your success, and create a new positive belief that will help lead you to success.

Inaccurate Belief	How it hurts me	How I would like it to be.	New Belief
Example: I need to devote all my time to my family because I have a new baby.	It hurts me because I spend all my time doing things for others but I do nothing for myself. Because of this, I am tired, stressed and unhappy at times.	I love my baby and family, but I want to also have some time to take care of myself and do things I enjoy. That would help me feel happier and decrease my stress.	It is important and healthy for me to devote time to myself, as well as to my family.

VICTORY LIST WORKSHEET

"Me Museum"

Review your life since childhood and make a list of your life victories. Do not think about how big or small they may have been. Instead, think about how great you felt when each happened. Use this sheet by reviewing your list periodically and right before you need a boost in confidence.

1	
2	
3	
4	
5	
6	
7	
8	

CHAPTER 5

GET STARTED

Well, the time has arrived! Are you ready? You are now more positive, you know exactly what you want and you have increased your confidence and motivation! If there is a bit of fear, push it aside for now (we will address that in chapter eight).

Everything has a beginning, and it doesn't matter how it happened or why it happened, just that it happened. The only way to start something is by taking some type of action. If you know what you want, you can start taking steps to do it. If you haven't narrowed it down yet, or if you require more information or training to get started, start researching or talking to those who know how to do it right now. One small step is all it takes to get you on your way. A baby bird has to summon the courage to take a step and fly…and so do you. In this chapter, I will show you some great techniques to ensure you progress forward toward your dreams.

Take small steps.
Have you heard the adage, "Rome wasn't built in a day"? Well, I have my own way of interpreting that saying. A large city full of completed stone structures and roads did not just appear on a plot of land overnight. It was built over time, little by little, step by step. But imagine if the builders started to build, looked at the pile of rock, worried they would never finish even one complete structure, and then quit. There would only be a pile of stone. Not only did it take many small actions to make one structure, but also many of the same actions had to be completed over and over again to create an entire city. Each time a new structure was built by the same people, it became a little easier and probably a little faster. After

building many structures, the builders became experts in what they were doing, even if they did not know much at all about what they were doing the first time around. They learned from their mistakes and tried different ways of doing things by altering their process or their product. That is exactly how you will reach your goals. Don't expect to do a day's work and wake up the next day to find instant success. It would be great, but it does not usually happen that way. Build your dreams one rock at a time, and you will progress step by step down the beautiful path toward your own Rome.

When your goal is broken into many smaller steps, it is much easier to start. You will not feel overwhelmed, and you will be less likely to give up before you even start. There are many techniques to help you create achievable goals.

Reverse your way to success.
One technique to break things down is what I call mosaic journey. To make a mosaic, each beautiful piece of glass is placed on a surface one by one to create an even more beautiful masterpiece when all the small pieces are in the correct place. It sounds simple, right? But before the tiny pieces can be placed on the surface, the glass has to be created. But there is even more. The correct chemical process is necessary to form the glass. Sand is needed before the chemical process can take place, and so on. Although I left out many individual steps, you can see that once we back away from the finished product, there are many more individual steps required before the mosaic can be complete.

Using this reverse method, you can take your large goal and imagine you've achieved it. Keep asking yourself the following question, "What did I need to do to get here?" Keep going backwards until you have all the steps in reverse from the final result to your smallest actions.

One personal example was when I first had the goal to publish children's books. I had never done it before, so I initially imagined I had the published books in my hands, and then I traced the steps in reverse. I needed to print the book to have a physical book, I needed to get a publisher to get the book to print. I needed to have illustrations to go with my words. I needed to write the words to have a story. I needed to have an idea for a story before I could write the words, and so on. This process breaks each piece into smaller, more achievable pieces, which will allow you to achieve your large goal without being overwhelmed or quitting!

Continuing with the book example, each one of the steps I already mentioned can be reversed even more to break smaller goals down into steps that can be achieved even if you are up all night with a baby, working, attending school or doing all three! Reverse to what is needed to reach the success level for your own unique circumstances. For example, the small goal of creating the idea may be broken down into reading a few children's books to see how other authors write, reading a blog about creating storylines, and reading a book about writing a children's book. Those goals can be reversed even further into fifteen-minute time frames, such as reading one children's book a day for three days, reading one blog post a day for three days, etc.

Continue to reverse until you create steps that are possible for you to fit into your schedule every day and you will ensure success. It may be helpful if you have an extra hour to work on goals, but in this busy world, you can also reach your goal at any pace you choose, as long as you keep slowly and steadily moving forward. Remember that important point. Keep slowly and steadily moving forward! This is the key to success. In chapters six and seven, you will learn tips that will help you create more physical and mental time in your day so you can keep moving forward!

Create a "Mind Map."
Another way to break your goal into steps is to use mind mapping. You may already know about mind mapping. There are many different ways to create mind maps. I create mind maps by drawing a circle in the middle of a paper and writing my main goal inside of the circle. After that, I draw lines extending out from the large circle and connect them to smaller circles that I draw. I write the smaller goals that need to be completed to achieve the larger goal inside those circles. I continue to do this for each circle until there are many smaller and smaller circles and I cannot

think of any more steps that are needed. The smallest circles become your starting points that eventually help you reach your main goal. Use the *Mind Map Worksheet* at the end of the chapter or a sheet of paper to create your own Mind Map. Remember to break your tasks down to the level that you can easily complete in your allotted time frame, so you will be able to fit your task into your very busy day and continue to move forward. Even if a task takes longer, for example, watching a one-hour learning video, you can break it into small segments if necessary.

While going through the process of breaking down goals, you could determine that your original goal is something you would like to pursue, find something else you want to pursue you were not originally aware of, or decide you do not want to pursue this interest at all. Regardless of your discovery, you are making progress and experiencing greater clarity while also learning more about yourself and the topic you choose. It's a win-win situation for you! Your confidence and knowledge will increase and you will feel a sense of accomplishment just by getting started!

Create an action plan.
Once you have used the reverse method or the mind map method to break your goals into the smallest pieces possible, fill out the *Action Plan Worksheet* at the end of the chapter. Start by listing your first task. The plan will guide you through the process of deciding whether the task will be completed by you or by someone else, any resources needed, any perceived obstacles to overcome, and the desired completion date. There is also a column for documenting task completion. This worksheet will help you plan and review your progress. Start writing in your first tasks and get ready to set aside time to take action.

Make a time commitment.
If you stop for a moment and think of all the successful people you have ever read or heard about, ask yourself this one question: Did they sit home with an idea in their head or did they, in some way decide to take action? Can you commit to

arranging an extra 15-20 minutes today or tomorrow, even if you have to take a shorter lunch, get up a few minutes earlier, check your phone less often or go to bed a few minutes later? I can assure you it will be worth it. If life intervenes, don't get upset. Smile, take a deep breath, count your blessings, schedule another time and get started again. Once you reach your goal, I can guarantee you will ask yourself, "Why didn't I do this long ago?" So, I will say this for the last time, *start now*! Put a smile on your face, sit up tall and declare, "The time is now!" Say it once more like you really mean it. How do you feel? I know you can do this. I believe in you. Just give it a try and see how great it feels!

Set your start date.
Setting a start date may sound like common sense, but it is often one of the primary reasons people don't accomplish their goals. They think a better time to start will come along, so they never take the first step. Make it official; put it in your calendar with reminders for a day or two before you start. That prepares you mentally and can build excitement. Ideally, your first task should be able to be completed in 15 minutes or less. This will ensure you take that first step. Don't, and I mean don't, get stuck planning and planning some more.

Pick a number!
Now that you have taken the first step, I want you to know about some other tips that will get you closer and closer to your desired results. One tip is to pick a number from 2-5. Commit to completing that number of steps each and every day to create the baby steps needed to start the path to your larger goals. Mark off each step on your action plan after completing it. Having a set number of tasks to complete each day will keep you moving forward, and you will be amazed at what larger results will come out of the small things you do, even at a much later date.

For example, when I was writing my children's book, I decided to do five things a day to market my book. I would do things like sending out tweets, making new LinkedIn connections, sending emails, and sometimes setting up a quick social media contest or giveaway. These were things I could do throughout my busy day. For a while, I wasn't seeing any results from my work, but I kept at it.

Suddenly, things started to happen. I received an email, which I almost deleted, inviting me to submit a proposal to write a children's book for the CDC. I received a headshot of a famous musician in the mail who was interested in helping spread my message. I received a return email from a PBS executive, which included his direct phone number and a message that he was available to talk to me about my project. I received a signed thank you card from Hilary Clinton for sending her one of my books following the birth of her grandchild, and I was featured in a case study, which included a financial award. All this came from making five small gestures each day.

It started to feel like my birthday every day! I never knew what I would see when I opened my email, checked my mailbox or took a phone call, all because I consistently completed 5 small tasks a day with no expectations of anything coming from them, and then I put them out of my mind. Soon, it became much more fun to do the five simple tasks because I never knew what surprises could be lurking around the corner, ready to jump out and shower me with excitement! Reach out, tell people what you're doing, promote on social media, contact possible mentors, or do anything you want to do that may help you in reaching your goal, then forget about it and step back and enjoy the unexpected results when you least expect them!

Be accountable.
Here is a tip that will help you achieve and keep you on track, even on those days that you may want to give up. Find an accountability associate. There is no better way to achieve something than to know that someone else is going to ask you if you followed through with what you said you were going to do! It can be a friend, a member of an Internet group you belong to, a partner, a parent, or a personal or business coach.

To use this technique, make your actions specific and measurable, for example, "I'm going to read five blog posts about how to teach an online course for profit, then document that I completed this task in an email to my accountability associate by Wednesday at 5pm." That way, your accountability associate will be able to quickly determine if you achieved that goal. I have to confess, there have been times when I really had to hustle because I waited until the last minute to do what I promised, but I wanted to save face by telling my accountability associate that I completed it rather than not keep my word. Keep in mind that there are emergency situations and family situations that can pop up and prevent you from completing a goal on time, and that is totally understandable. An accountability associate is there to hold you accountable, but not to make you feel bad if you do not make your commitment. A good accountability associate will cheer you on when you succeed and provide tips and words of encouragement that will help you complete your goal.

If you don't already have an accountability associate, you may find one as you begin to share your achievements and goals with others. If someone gets excited for you or mentions they always thought about doing the same thing you are doing, ask them if they would like to help you stay accountable. You could offer to return the favor. If you are interested in receiving professional accountability services complete the contact form and request more information at www.beAmastermom.com.

Surround yourself with inspiration.
It is helpful to surround yourself with people who are doing something similar. You will inspire each other and trade important tips and information. You may be thinking, "How can I add a group meeting to my busy day?" Well, it doesn't have to be an additional group and you don't have to spend a lot of time doing this.

It could be an Internet group in your field of interest. Internet groups are really easy to find when searching Facebook groups. For instance, if you are interested in being a photographer, search Facebook for photography groups. You can even find groups that are specific to the type of photos you are interested in taking, such as nature or newborns, etc. Please be cautious if you select this method. Don't provide too much identifying information, use judgment and be safe while in Internet groups with those you do not know. I belong to authors groups and entrepreneur groups, and I have received invaluable information and connections to people all over the world while interacting within my groups.

You can also find people with similar interests while having conversations with other parents at the playground, at a playgroup, at a parent-child resource center, at a school or daycare. If you do have additional time once a month or more, you could start or join a meet-up group at your local library or coffee shop. There may also be a young professional group in your area. There are many ways to find others with similar interests and availability. The additional motivation you gain from others who support you, guide you and relate to you will keep you moving forward.

This is such an exciting and empowering time, and let me tell you why. When you get started, you are doing things that will help you in more ways than you can imagine. You are showing everyone around you that you are serious about reaching your goals, whether it's losing weight, running your first race, starting your own company or saving for a large purchase. People will start to notice your commitment and those who have similar goals but were afraid to talk about them may become attracted to you and your drive. I remember when I started telling others about writing my books; several people approached me and said things like, "I always wanted to do that too," and "How did you know what to do to get started?" You may inspire others to go for it too!

You will also begin to learn a bit more about yourself, your process and your chosen topic along the way and that will help you proceed even faster. You may get feedback and suggestions from others that can help you move forward. You may find that you have supporters and cheerleaders you never expected. As I began to meet some of my goals, there were times when so many people were praising me about my progress that I began to feel slightly embarrassed at how much I was accomplishing and at the attention I was getting! This was a challenge to me because of a limiting belief about modesty that I once held and have since successfully overcome. As you continually work on your goals, you will become more accountable, worries and confusion that you had will clear, and you will begin to feel proud of yourself for each new step you take.

HOW GETTING STARTED HELPS YOUR CHILD

Share your excitement.
You are now taking action, feeling confident and wondering when that first great surprise will find you. You are happy and your child can feel it. Talk to your child. Share your excitement. If your child is an infant, it's ok, just talk away. Tell your story. Share all the details. Hold your baby as you share your excitement, and your baby will also watch your facial expressions. You will be showing excitement, happiness, maybe surprise and sometimes a little fear as you talk about your plan and how it felt to take action. You will feel great by sharing the exciting decisions and actions in your life, even if your baby can not comprehend what you are saying. Your baby will benefit from hearing the sounds, the words and the intonation in your voice. Your baby will love the back and forth talks with you. Your baby will enjoy your attention. Your baby will engage with you and your smiles, and this will not only promote brain development but may distract your baby from other sensations, such as tiredness, hunger, or gas. These back and forth interactions are not only fun but also important to your baby's overall development. Wow, what a great experience for your child to take part in.

If your child is older, the information in this chapter about how taking action can lead to success can be one of the best lessons to learn. Share your excitement with your child. Discuss your plans at the dinner table and maybe even celebrate your start date with a special meal or dessert. Let you child see the excitement you feel about working toward your goal. Discuss goals your child may have and encourage your child to get excited and to join you by working toward their own goal at the same time. When your child is excited about their goals, they will be more likely to reach their intended results.

Be a role model.
The steps you learned in this chapter about surrounding yourself with those who have the same goals and breaking down very large goals to small achievable steps are techniques that will also benefit your child for a lifetime. When you model these techniques, your child will get to actually see how successful the techniques are while in action. Your child will learn that taking action is the first step to achieving anything. Knowing, observing and developing this mindset will teach your child that anything is possible, whether it is finding a way to get money to buy a piece of candy or convincing their school to offer guitar classes. Encourage your child to set goals, select a time to start and take action.

Help your child get started.
Help your child select a goal they want to achieve. Brainstorm ideas with them if they do not have a goal in mind. Once your child selects a goal, ask if they thought about the steps they will take to reach that goal. Help them plan how they will break their goal down into smaller and smaller pieces. Teach them how to break goals down into small, easily-achieved parts because small consistent steps will propel them on their way. This can be done with children of all ages. Older children can be introduced to mind mapping, reversing their way to success, and action plans, but even very young children can be taught this concept. One example for a young child would be to have the child help clean up toys from the yard. Start by explaining to your child that they will help clean the yard by taking little steps. First ask your child to pick up two items and put them away as you watch to make sure they don't get out more! A while later, have your child go

back outside and pick up two more toys, then continue this process until the yard is clean. Praise your child for getting the whole yard clean and explain that by taking small steps, they can do big things.

Teach your child about accountability.
Share the tasks you are working on with your family. It can be a fun dinner conversation. Let your family know when you plan to complete a task and ask them to remind you at dinner to see if you completed it as planned. This will help you be accountable and will model accountability to your child.

Explain to your child that at times, it may be difficult to stay on task when working toward a goal. Explain that by telling others, it helps you to be more accountable and helps keep you on track. Ask your child if they want to let you know when they are working on completing a task so you can ask them if they completed it successfully to keep them accountable. Explore other ways to be accountable such as writing the task on a sticky note on the refrigerator or telling a friend. Your child may find it easier to reach a goal if they have a friend or sibling who is also working on a similar goal.

Discuss why inspiration is important.
While discussing your goals at the dinner table or while sitting with your family, thank them for being interested and asking you about your progress toward your goals. Explain that this inspires you to work hard toward your goal. Talk about any other ways you are being inspired such as mutual groups or someone you know who is working toward a similar goal. Explain that surrounding yourself with people who support you or with others working toward similar goals helps you reach your goal. Explore with your child ways they can do the same.

You are on your way to helping your child develop great success habits by modeling the steps to goal attainment. You are also helping your child understand that by breaking goals down into easily achievable pieces, taking consistent action, being accountable and finding support from others who believe in their goals, even goals that may at first seem impossible can be achieved.

GET STARTED REVIEW

1. Just do it! The best way to reach any goal is to take action. It doesn't have to be perfect, it doesn't have to be final, and it doesn't have to have complete clarity; just do it. All the planning, worrying, and researching in the world will not get you to your dreams the way taking action will!

2. Your Mosaic Journey, also described as reversing your way to success, is a process where you take your main goal and then take a step backwards. Ask yourself, "What did I need to do to get here?" Keep backing up until you have broken your goal down into small, achievable steps.

3. Mind mapping is a process used by many. Start by writing your main goal inside a circle in the middle of a sheet of paper then draw lines extending from the main circle and connect them to smaller circles. Inside the smaller circles, write the things you have to do to get to the goal in the larger circle. Repeat the process with each circle that you draw until you have every step broken down into the smallest tasks. Your small outer circles will contain the smallest tasks you will complete first.

4. Creating an action plan will help you plan and review the progress you are making toward your goal.

5. Talking about your goal will make people realize you are serious. The more you talk about it, the more feedback, information and support you will receive. You will inspire others. You will become accountable. You will feel proud once you have started the journey toward achieving your dream.

6. Taking 2-5 small steps each day will make large dreams come true. Taking small consistent steps is an easy way to not get overwhelmed and will lead you straight to your end goal. Remember, good things will come from doing this!

7. Being accountable will ensure you reach your goal. Knowing that someone else is there to inspire you and to check on your progress can be just what you need to keep moving consistently in the right direction.

8. Surround yourself with others who support and encourage you. Consider people you can learn from. Connect with them and tell them what you are doing. Expand your horizons in any way you can.

Get Started Exercises

1. Look at your list of goals and select the goal you would most like to achieve.

2. Use either Reverse Success Method or the *Mind Map Worksheet* to break your large goal down into many small achievable goals. Remember to consider your time schedule as you do this and break each goal down into very small tasks.

3. Once you have your goal broken down into the smallest tasks possible, fill out the *Action Plan Worksheet* by listing the steps you will take, using it as a guide to task completion.

4. Select a start date. Select your first task and just do it! Don't forget to review your *Victory List Worksheet* from chapter four to get excited and to feel more confident, if needed.

5. Congratulate yourself! You are on your way to achieving your dreams.

6. Complete the number of tasks you decided to complete every day.

7. Share your excitement with others.

8. Select an accountability associate or group.

9. Connect with others who have similar interests who are also working towards achieving goals or have already achieved them.

10. Feel grateful that by taking action, both you and your child will benefit.

Get Started Exercises to Help Your Child

1. Share the excitement of starting (taking action) with your child regardless of age.

2. When introducing the concepts in this chapter, keep activities aligned with your child's development and level of understanding.

3. Explore desires or outcomes your child may be excited about achieving. When your child is excited about the outcomes, they will achieve the best results.

4. Introduce the concept of goals and breaking goals down. For example, picking up one toy, then another for a young child, on up to mind mapping and action plans for an older child.

5. Help an older child make a commitment, plan a time to get started, pick a set number of small tasks to do each day and be accountable by working with a friend or relative.

MIND MAP WORKSHEET

1. Write your main goal in the center circle then work backwards.
2. The steps you need to take to get to the main goal become the sub goals.
3. Write the sub goals in the smaller circles.
4. Continue this process outward until you have broken each goal into the smallest pieces possible. You may prefer a large sheet of poster board.
5. Draw more circles and lines as needed.
6. You can find mind map software and examples of mind maps online.

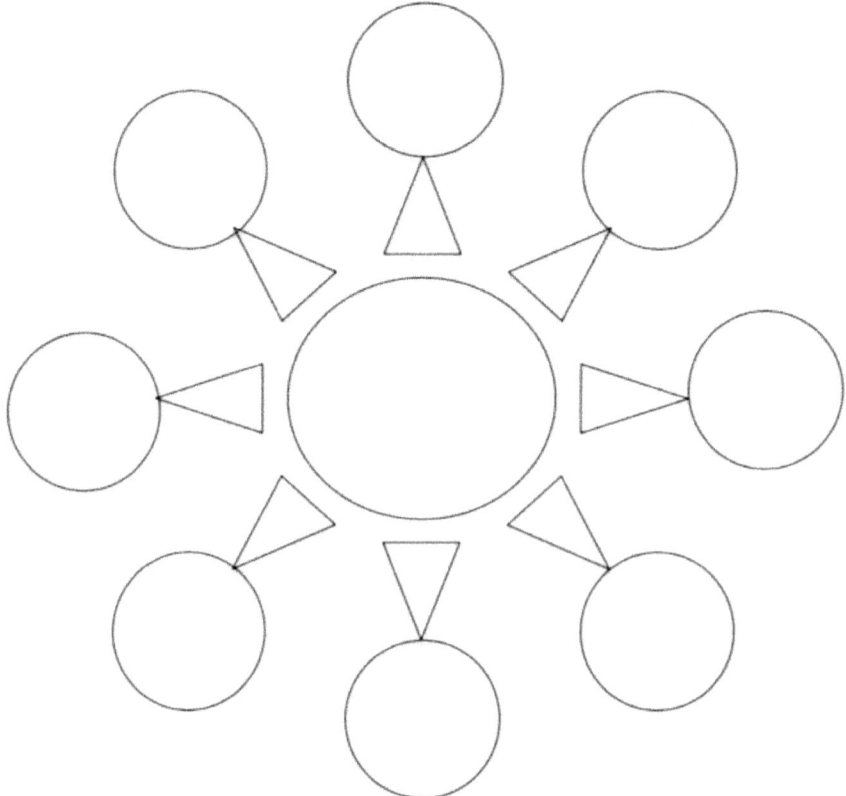

ACTION PLAN WORKSHEET

After working backwards and breaking your large goal down into the smallest bits possible, take the smallest sub goal and list it on this worksheet. When you have completed the first sub goal move on to the next. Use one worksheet for each sub goal you are working on.

My Goal:_____

Action steps	Who will complete this step?	Resources needed	Obstacles to overcome and plan	Desired completion date	Complete? Yes/No
1.					
2.					
3.					
4.					
5.					

CHAPTER 6

FIND TIME

It happens. Your life is moving along, you have children, and you find your life is extra busy. It feels like you have no time for anything. I can sum that experience up in one funny memory that I have, and I remember the exact moment I had that realization.

One day, I was picking my children up from the daycare center after work. My best friend, who I did everything with, was in the parking spot next to me. We were both loading our tired children in our cars. My friend had recently moved to a nearby town, and due to our increasingly busy lives, we didn't get to see each other as often. While loading our children into our cars, and between the cries and the commotion, we tried to schedule a date to get together. It went kind of like this as we went back and forth trying to schedule time together…

"How about Thursday after work?"

"I have no free time that day."

"How about Saturday?"

"Nope I'm booked up all day. Sunday?"

"I don't have one free minute on Sunday."

After a few tries and a few cries from very impatient kids, I jokingly said, "Well, looks like I'll see you after high school graduation." We laughed and drove off. I wish I knew then the time tricks I know now, because the time I spent with my friend became less and less, and it didn't have to be that way.

Learn to say no.

That scenario does not have to happen to you if you use the easy time hacks I am about to tell you. The first hack consists of one simple word that is often a toddler's favorite word, but it can be a difficult word for adults. You can probably guess that word already!

The word is *no*. Think about it, toddlers love to be independent and they exercise that right often by saying no to just about everything. Independence is an important stage of development. You most likely went through the no stage when you were a toddler too. Well, what happened over all those years, to change how easy it was to say no? Let's think about it. You may have found out that by saying no, you hurt someone's feelings. Teachers or parents may have said you *had* to do it anyway, or maybe you can even remember a time you were punished because you said no and didn't do something others thought you should have done. After having many similar experiences, you eventually said no less and less. You stopped thinking about what would make you happy and started to react by what you thought was right, would keep you out of trouble or would make others happy. Well, now you are an adult, and it is time to change your thinking regarding that little but mighty word.

Here are some things to consider when you are asked a yes/no question. First, you can always take time to think about it. Just say, "It sounds great; let me check into it," or "I'd love to help, but let me review my schedule and get back to you."

Another way to say no is to explain that you really love the idea, cause, invitation and so on, and you would love to help, but you have been so overbooked lately that you made a sincere commitment to spend more time with your family, your children, on your project, or whatever it is you are trying to devote more time to. Explain that you realize their request sounds wonderful, but it's really important for you to stick with your commitment right now. If you are sincere, most people will understand and even respect your decision. If they do not, they are not being supportive. Remind yourself that this is a step you need to take if you are going to increase your happiness and reach your goals. Most times, you will be surprised at how easy it can be to say no, and the reaction you receive from others is not half as bad as you imagine it will be.

Another thing to remember is that someone else's poor planning should not create an emergency for you. I remember one time when I received a call one afternoon at work. It was an invitation to go to dinner that evening for a small impromptu birthday celebration that was taking place. I had just finished telling a co-worker how this was the only evening I would be home all week and how much I needed it and was really looking forward to it. Not knowing what to do and feeling caught off-guard, I accepted the invitation and hung up the phone in a really bad mood. It wasn't that I didn't appreciate the invitation; I was just tired and was looking forward to my relaxing evening at home. My co-worker asked why I had accepted, and I answered saying, "I did not want to hurt my neighbor's feelings." She then asked why I didn't explain the truth. I explained that the last thing I wanted to do was upset my neighbor and hurt her feelings. My co-worker reminded me that since it really was a last-minute request, it was not unrealistic that I would have other plans, so if I explained that to my neighbor, she should understand. At that moment, I decided she was right and with a very heavy feeling in the pit of my stomach, I called my neighbor back and explained the circumstances. She totally understood and in a matter of minutes, I was suddenly feeling much more at ease and again looking forward to my relaxing evening at home with my family. Since that day, I have practiced saying no to many other things that I used to always say yes to, and because of that one little change, I feel much more in control of my life!

Other ways to respond to a request without saying no may be to offer advice or refer the person to someone else who can help them. Some people explain that they don't have the finances or they have family obligations, a full calendar or something else that has to get done soon. Often, the person can relate to your circumstances and will react much better than you imagine they would. So, don't create more angst on your own; just say no.

Many of the world's top leaders and professionals say no many times a day. This gives them the time to work on the things that bring them success, instead of working on everything. It is ok to say it. It is a highly developed skill, so start practicing today and see how much easier it becomes.

Start practicing saying no today. Say no to little things and work your way up to the larger refusals. For example, to start, try saying no when you're really tired and your partner asks you to watch a TV movie you have already seen five times, or when your little one asks for one more piece of candy. Start small and only say no if you really mean it, not just for the sake of practice, and remember you do need to have a fun balanced life, so don't count out everything just to create more time. Once you get a bit of practice, work your way up to larger refusals, and don't forget to use some of the tips in this chapter.

Identify time wasters.
When you eliminate time-wasting activities and give priority each day to your efforts that are the most productive, you will begin to notice a big difference. Begin to focus on the daily activities that will provide the greatest results, instead of the less productive things you do each day.

An example of a time waster that I identified was when I used to tidy up the living room after putting the kids down for a nap each day. They would immediately get the same items out when they woke up, so I would have to pick up a second time each day. Once I eliminated that task, I created an additional 15 minutes a day. I bet you can think of things you do that are not really necessary. Often, it is an internal adjustment to something we have been doing for a very long time without giving it much thought. Sometimes, you may just want to stop the task all together.

You can determine which tasks you need to decrease or stop doing by completing the *Time Waster Worksheet* at the end of this chapter. As you prepare to compete the worksheet, you will need to pay close attention to activities or tasks you do on a routine basis. You will then document the activities you spend time on, and the amount of time you spend on each activity. You can do this for several days. Include weekdays, evenings and weekends. After you do this, follow the process of determining the level of return for each activity by deciding if this activity is highly productive, moderately productive or less productive for you. You will then fill in the last column of the worksheet with the words Delete, Share, Swap, or Reassess by deciding to either delete the task entirely, share it with someone else, or swap it for something you like to do or with someone who can help you do it quicker. You can also write in the word Reassess, if you want to reevaluate your decision after trying it for a few days to make sure it is working the way you had hoped. These terms will be discussed in greater detail later in this chapter.

Once you complete the worksheet, you will be able to easily calculate the additional time available for working on your goals or just having some "me" time.

Focus on your most productive tasks.
Look to see where you can increase time spent on tasks that will get you closer to your goal. If there are tasks you can decrease in order to allow you to increase the tasks that are getting you closer to your goal, do that now. Try it for a few days, re-evaluate and continue to adjust until you create the time you need to succeed.

I found that even though it was important for me to check email and market with social media, the task that would propel me toward my goal the most was completing my current book. Well, I have to admit, at times I can be easily distracted by my technology. Can you relate to this scenario? (True funny side note: As I was editing this book, I looked down at my phone right before editing the above sentence about being distracted by technology! Luckily, I used the tip I'm about to tell you, laughed at myself and got right back to work without skipping a beat!)

Most phones have a handy timer, which is usually found by selecting the clock icon. If yours does not, there are many free timer apps available. The timer actually saves me time by consolidating my important tasks into a set 100% focused time period. This provides encouragement by allowing me to visually see how much time is left.

Here is what happens when I do not use the timer. I hear the notification sound that I have received a message on my phone and check it out. After responding to the message, I notice that I have several Twitter or Facebook messages. Of course, I decide to just quickly read and respond to them and before I know it, I've viewed and interacted with many posts and tweets. Next, I decide that I might as well check my email, and I start deleting my unimportant emails until I find one containing a link to a blog post with a very catchy title, and I'm off...and on and on and on.

This exact scenario was why I made the decision that while writing this book, I would use the timer on my phone to create uninterrupted periods of time. It helps by allowing me to schedule small chunks of highly focused time, and it reminds me of the progress I have already made and the short amount of time I have left before I can take a break. Even if I have an important email regarding one of my goals, it will still be there in thirty minutes, and I get my planned work done too!

Another tip that works even better, is leaving my phone in another room and only checking it three times a day. I created unique ringtones or notification sounds for those who have me listed as an emergency contact, and I make sure I can hear my phone from the other room. Once I started planning my schedule by giving the most focus to my most productive tasks, I received much faster and better outcomes.

Learn to delegate and ask for help.
Another great way to create extra time in your day is to delegate tasks to others. Maybe you don't need to be the only person who walks the dog or feeds the cat each day. If there are others at work or home that you can delegate tasks to, give it a try. Your five-year-old may actually enjoy scooping up a cup of cat food and pouring it into the bowl for the cat each day at dinnertime. It also teaches your child to be responsible, and it may cause them to feel proud of themselves for helping out at home.

Sometimes, you benefit by asking others to help you. You can ask a partner, a family member or a friend for help, but just remember, as you learned earlier in the chapter, sometimes it's ok if they tell you no. Often, people are willing to help when they have time and are asked nicely. It helps to sincerely point out why it may be a good idea for the other person to help you, for example, "I've noticed how Gia really loves when you read to her. Would you read her a book after dinner each day so I can complete one daily step toward my goal?" Give it a try!

Find ways to swap and share tasks.
You do not have to do everything, and you should not do everything yourself. If you observe someone else who has a task you enjoy or do well, and you have a task you do not know how to do or do not enjoy doing, make a swap. Do this by making an offer to help someone else in return for the task you don't like or don't know how to do. Once I wanted help on a computer project I was working on and a friend needed help with a book she was writing, so I helped her and she helped me, and we were both successful at reaching our goal without putting in the additional time it would have taken us to research and learn the things we did not know about the task we needed to complete. By doing that, neither of us had to spend extra time learning or extra money to pay someone to do it for us.

If the task is large, such as taking your children to school each day, you can share that task with a neighbor who is doing the same thing. You could take turns each day or switch off weekly or monthly. This would create additional time for both of you and over a period of a year, that time really accumulates. This would also work for mutual activities or even cooking and freezing meals for each other! If you brainstorm, you may come up with many unique options.

Be an expert multitasker.
Another way to create extra time is to safely double up tasks when possible. If something you may need to do to help you reach a goal is to learn more about a topic or increase your motivation or both, an easy way to do this is to listen to free podcasts while you're safely doing another task. For example, if your goals include becoming healthier and learning about website creation, you could spend your lunch break at work eating some fruit and listening to a podcast about website development. You could clean the house while listening to audio about ways to successfully market on social media or you could create a great name for your business while taking a shower or drying your hair. Be creative, and you will find the hidden time within your day.

Review your day each night.
One more hack that has created time and clarity for me is an end-of-day review. Every night as I lay in bed, I review the day and ask myself these questions: On a scale of 1-10, how would I rate my day? How would I rate the productivity of my day? What could I have done better? How could I have been more productive? What are the top 2-3 things I will achieve tomorrow that will put me even closer to my goal? Sometimes, I simply fill out a review worksheet. The *Daily Review Worksheet* at the end of this chapter will take you through the steps to adequately review your daily progress. It's kind of like giving yourself a mini work review or report card, and it helps you get clarity about what works and what doesn't as you plan daily improvement. It also saves you time because you won't have to spend the first 15 minutes of your productive time deciding what to work on. You can just quickly start your day. Another benefit of daily review is that your subconscious mind will take over while you sleep, and who knows, you may even dream about a solution or a new idea!

Begin to create positive new habits that will help you use your time more wisely.

When you are able to stay on top of things, you are better able to avoid time wasting consequences. For example, taking care of car maintenance on a scheduled routine basis may prevent costly time-eating emergencies from happening, and setting your cellphone timer each time you work will help you maintain your focus. Multiple research studies indicate that it is necessary to practice a task routinely for approximately one to two months to establish a habit, so don't give up too soon! I usually find that when I plan to establish a new routine it gets easier to maintain after about one week of consistent effort. By the time I reach one month, things go smoothly and by two months, I start to feel guilty if I take a day off!

Replace your bad habits.
Even better than creating a new habit, double up by replacing a bad habit with a good habit and save precious time! You know the bad habits I'm talking about. Does this sound familiar? Putting things off until it turns into a time-consuming crisis,

wasting productive time by constantly checking social media, not staying organized, saying "I'll start completing a daily review tomorrow" and "I'll save for my house/car/children's education later." It is often hard to stop an old habit and start a new one, but replacing the old habit with a new habit is a bit easier. Remember, it becomes much easier the longer you consistently practice doing it.

Start adding one good habit at a time.
When you replace bad habits with good habits, it is best to start with just one habit at a time so you can devote more attention to it and you don't feel overwhelmed. You may need reminders at first, so set reminders on your phone, on your computer, hang signs, set alarms, and do whatever you need to do to remind yourself. Take a minute to remind yourself why it is important to create the new habit. What is the outcome you hope to achieve? If you wanted to spend 15 minutes every day working on a project, create a checklist and set up a routine to do it every day at the same time, and don't make excuses. Start the new habit you want to establish whether you feel like it at that moment or not, because after a few minutes of working, you will start to feel better about it. Once the 15 minutes is complete, you will feel proud of yourself for sticking to it. After doing this over and over again for about one month, I promise you, you will start to feel bad if you don't do it! Make the commitment, do it and know it will get easier!

To sum up this important chapter, and to help you create time to work on your goals or just get a little extra time for yourself, I will review and include a few examples of how you can find more time. Get up a half-hour earlier, go to bed a half-hour later, or extend your day by 15 minutes each morning and night. Swap a half-hour of childcare a day or an hour every other day with a friend or neighbor who is also working toward their goals or just wants to support you. If your child is older and attends activities, take something along you can do while waiting. Prepare the night before for the next day. Not only does being prepared make for a less hectic morning, but it can create additional time that can be used for other things, instead of searching for misplaced items or making last-minute decisions. You've got this! Keep brainstorming. You are on your way.

HOW FINDING TIME HELPS YOUR CHILD

Using time-saving tips will create more time for you to spend with your family and allow you to work toward your goals. Your child will receive more one-on-one time with you, and that can lead to increased happiness for both of you. Don't forget to spend some of your newly organized time sharing a fun activity with your family or spending time talking with your child about your child's favorite topics. You will feel better and your stress level will decrease. So, return to your *Time Waster Worksheet* and *Daily Review Worksheet* often so you can maximize the time you spend with your family too.

Help your child use time wisely.
If your child is having difficulty finding time to finish a task, explore ways to create more time. A discussion involving the search for time wasters may be beneficial. If you discuss this topic with your child and point out some of your own time wasters you are currently working on or have corrected, it may help your child better understand what a time waster is and make them less likely to feel you are accusing them of unnecessarily wasting time. Ask your child if it may help them to do something similar and share any tips you are currently using such as phone timers or time savers. Ask your child if they can think of any other time wasters you may be doing and ask if they would like you to do the same for them. Sometimes, a fresh set of eyes can see things that you cannot.

Explore healthy and unhealthy habits.
As your child observes you working on developing good habits instead of continuing unhealthy habits, discuss your progress

regarding the habits. This can develop into a great family discussion with an older child. You can talk about how you made the decision that something you were doing was not as good for you, so you decided to create a new healthy habit to replace the not-so-good habit. You can explain how it can be difficult at first, but over time and with consistent practice, it gets easier, just like playing a new sport, a musical instrument or sometimes, even doing homework. You can ask your child if there is anything they would like to do differently; work together to help each other create a new good habit. This discussion can even start at a young age. For example, you can explain to your young child why putting their shoes by the door each evening can save time in the morning, and explain that if they did it every day at the same time, it would become much easier to remember to do. Make a chart and let them mark it each evening to see how long it takes before they easily remember to put their shoes by the door on their own. You can use a chart to help your child develop other healthy habits too. For an older child who has trouble getting out the door on time in the morning, you may have a discussion about developing a habit of gathering all their homework and school supplies and setting out their clothes before they go to bed. You can then help them evaluate how that is working, if any adjustments are needed and if over time, it is getting easier for them to do.

Double up chores and fun.
You can also show your child how to combine tasks and do activities such as cleaning their room while listening to their favorite music or watching their favorite video, in order to make time for something else that they want to do, or just to make the task more enjoyable. Explain that this is ok to do as long it can be safely done, but it is not a good idea when working on serious tasks like homework or studying.

Integrate a daily review.
You can use the daily review process in a less formal way with your child at the dinner table as you discuss the events of their

day. If a difficult event took place that day, such as an argument with a friend or a bullying event, you could review it with them by asking if they could do it over again, would there be anything they could think of that they would do differently. You could then help them brainstorm ideas that could have been helpful, that they may not have thought of. Explain to them that this is a good way to learn new things about themselves and others, and also to continually improve and learn from their experiences.

You can also use this process when good things happen. Explore the good things that happened that day, discuss the events that led up to them and ways to continue to experience the same or similar situations. For example, if your child came home and said they received a compliment from the principal for setting up the chairs in the cafeteria, congratulate them for volunteering and helping to set up the chairs and ask them why they set up the chairs. If they reply their teacher asked for volunteers and they raised their hand, you can have the discussion about how volunteering at school was a good choice and suggest that it may be a good idea to volunteer to help the next time their teacher asks also.

The tips in this chapter will not only help you, but they will help your child become aware of different ways to create additional time, make some tasks more enjoyable, and replace unhealthy habits with healthy habits. Your child will also learn that everyone can benefit from continual evaluation and improvement, no matter how well they do something the first time, and that it can also save time. Introduce these tips at appropriate times and in age-appropriate ways. It is a good idea to introduce the topic of time-saving tips to your child before your child begins to struggle with a time challenge, but reminding your child about the tips and reinforcing them when your child is experiencing a challenge can also help them remember to use the tips in similar situations.

FIND TIME REVIEW

1. Saying no can be beneficial. It is something many of the world's top leaders and successful professionals have learned to do very well.
2. When you eliminate time-wasting activities and give priority each day to your efforts that are most productive, you will reach your goals faster.
3. Learning to delegate and ask for help when needed can free up valuable time.
4. Finding ways to swap and share chores with others can increase productivity or create extra free time.
5. Safely doubling up tasks when possible can create additional time for working on other tasks.
6. Evaluating your day before you go to sleep by asking yourself the 5 simple questions on the *Daily Review Worksheet* will not only save you time the following day but will create clarity and continually improve your productivity.
7. Replacing a time-wasting bad habit with a productive good habit can free up valuable time and is best done when focusing on adding one habit at a time.
8. When you model and introduce some of these tips to your child, your child will get to benefit from extra one-on-one time with you, learn invaluable time- saving skills and experience the importance of forming good lifelong habits.

Find Time Exercises

1. Practice saying no without feeling guilty. Start with smaller or less important requests, and then work your way up to larger ones. Practice. Practice. Practice. You deserve time for your family and for yourself.

2. Keep a tally or a journal of the tasks you spend your time on every day for several days. Include day, evening and weekends. Fill out the *Time Waster Worksheet* and return to it periodically.

3. Review the *Time Waster Worksheet* and identify the tasks that are the most productive and create the largest amount of success. Focus on these tasks to determine the fastest path to reaching your goals.

4. Review the *Time Waster Worksheet* to identify the time suckers that are delaying your progress and taking away from maintaining a balanced life. Find ways to eliminate, decrease or replace these activities.

5. Delegate, ask, share and swap tasks when you can.

6. Double up on tasks when you can safely do so.

7. Fill out the five simple review questions on the *Daily Review Worksheet* at the end of each day. This will provide clarity, save you time and increase your productivity.

8. Replace one old time-wasting bad habit with one good new habit until it becomes routine, then move on to the next one. Be consistent, keep track and just do it. It will become easier the more persistent you are.

9. Create an extra half-hour or more each day by creatively following the tips in this chapter.

10. Spend the extra time you create reaching your goals and providing extra one-on- one time with your child.

11. Feel grateful that by creating extra time, both you and your child will benefit.

Find Time Exercises to Help Your Child

1. Share the time-saving tips with your child in simple ways as soon as your child is old enough to comprehend.

2. Explain to an older child how you made the decision that something you were doing was not really good for you, so you decided to create a new healthy habit to replace the not-so-good habit. Ask your child if there is anything they would like to do differently, then work together to create a new habit using visual reminders.

3. Show your child how to combine tasks in order to make time for something that they want to do or to make the task more enjoyable.

4. Use the daily review process in a less formal way with your child at the dinner table, as you discuss the events of their day. Brainstorm ways to approach similar situations in the future, when things didn't go well, and reinforce the positive approach used for things that did.

TIME WASTER WORKSHEET

As you go through your day, list each activity that you do. Does each activity help you reach your goals? Evaluate other ways to get high returns while creating additional time.

Activity	Time spent	Level of return	Delete, Swap, Share, Reassess	Time Created
Example: Social Media	2 hours/day	Medium	Decrease to 30 min 2x per day try a few days and REASSESS	5 hours/week
Example: Exercising	30 min/day	High	SWAP Play 30 min running game in yard with kids 2x week	1 hr/week by combining exercise with playtime

Now that you have documented your activities, go back and brainstorm the steps you will take to find more time to reach your goals and do what you love!

DAILY REVIEW WORKSHEET

Date _____

How would I rate my day overall?	1 2 3 4 5 6 7 8 9 10
How would I rate how productive my day was?	1 2 3 4 5 6 7 8 9 10
What could I have done better?	
How could I have been more productive?	
What are the top 2-3 things I will achieve tomorrow that will put me even closer to my goal?	

Now that you have evaluated your day and planned for tomorrow, take a minute to congratulate yourself for making progress and visualize how it will feel when you

CRUSH YOUR GOAL!

CHAPTER 7

GET ORGANIZED

If I asked several people what getting organized meant to them, I would get many answers. Some people may discuss tidying things up, others may think of planning or making lists and still others may think about completing tasks in a routine manner. All three of those ideas can lead to better organization, which in turn can lead to increased productivity in general. Here is an example of how keeping things tidy, planning and routines could have created a different outcome for this story.

A friend was telling me about her hectic morning. She had to deliver a large stage prop to her son's school for a play. She knew her car trunk was full of items she had placed in it over time and had never removed, such as sports equipment, gardening items and winter clothing. She knew she should have removed the items before it became too full, but she never got around to it. All week, she stressed about making room in her trunk. She planned several different times to clean it out, but when the time came, she was either tired or had something more important to do. She was finally going to empty the trunk the evening before she had to transport the prop, but she put it off again because it was dark outside. She decided she would do it in the morning when it was lighter. The next morning she woke up, got ready and carried the prop out by the car fifteen minutes before it was time to leave but when she looked for the key to unlock the car, she couldn't find it. She said she had always meant to make a routine of placing her keys in a designated spot every evening, but she never got around to it. To end a long story, she was stressed, her child was stressed, she was late driving her child to school and late for work. I'm sure most of us have had days like this. This is the kind of day that could have gone a bit smoother if we had just taken some time earlier to avert chaos. This example shows how getting organized is important for the purpose of being productive and decreasing stress.

CLEAN UP AND COMPLETE WHAT'S NOT DONE

How many times have you walked by that stack of mail, or that messy closet or the pile of shoes by the door and thought, "I have to take care of that really soon"? It may have even been something as simple as desk clutter, and in my case, it was!

Many times every day, I would walk by the kitchen desk and think, "I really need to clear that off." There was a pile of non-urgent mail, another pile of things to mail, and a pile of papers to go through in order to prepare my taxes. There was a stack of books I recently received in the mail and five of the proofs of the children's books I had written. I walked by that pile many times a day, day after day, and each time I looked at it, I felt stress.

The energy I was wasting from feeling stressed over my mess was taking my focus away from my other tasks, and it just didn't feel good. Finally, after weeks of walking by that messy desk, I took thirty minutes to go through the piles and clear up the desk, and it immediately changed the way I felt. I felt happy, relieved, and accomplished. It only took 30 minutes to clean up, compared to the accumulated hours of time I felt stressed as I walked by it each day. Now when I walk by, I look at the desk and feel good. Such a little thing can have such a big impact on the way we feel and the energy we are able to harness. Think about how good you felt the last time you did something similar.

We all face things we start and don't finish, and things that need our attention that we don't always get to. Sometimes, it may be because we aren't sure how to proceed, such as a broken garbage disposal. Sometimes, it can be overwhelming, like a very cluttered garage, and sometimes, we just don't feel we have time. But it has been shown that freeing your mind of the feelings that go along with the unfinished task can allow you to direct more energy toward other productive tasks. The more organized and complete you feel, the more focus you will be able to provide as you work toward your goals. Completion releases the energy-zapping stress that the unfinished task creates.

Try this exercise.
After you complete this chapter, look at the *Unfinished Business Worksheet* at the end of this chapter and take a walk around your house or apartment. What are the things you could easily complete? It may be the recyclables that have been building up, or the shovel you never put away from the storm four months ago or the clutter on the desk, just like I had. Now take a minute and complete the chore or clean up the mess. Check it off and then observe the energy you feel when you are done. If it is a really large chore or will take more time than you have available, fill in a scheduled completion date on the worksheet and commit to tackling it completely on the day selected. Once you do that, don't give it another thought because you have scheduled the completion process, so just imagine how great you will feel on that day, and walk right by. The next time you observe an unfinished task and can spare a minute, do it and see how it makes you feel. Larger tasks may have to be planned for a future date, and you may need help, but schedule them too. Then, instead of thinking, "Oh I need to take care of that," think, "I'm glad I've planned to do this!" You won't believe how good it will make you feel just to know you set aside a future date to tackle the task.

The same thing can happen when you are working toward your goals and they begin to pile up. When you use the methods you learned earlier in this book to break your goals into achievable chunks, there may be some tasks that you put off. As these tasks pile up and you stress about them day after day, they too are zapping energy that could be used to move forward. Figure out first why you haven't completed the tasks. Are you afraid to ask for help? Are you not sure how to proceed? Is the task something you just don't enjoy doing? Is the task too big? If you answer yes to any of those questions, then take the first step needed to make movement toward that goal. Maybe you need to read a post to learn how to do the step you are not sure about. Maybe you need to ask a friend or someone from a freelance website to do it for you. Maybe you have to break down the task even further, or maybe you have to ask yourself why you're afraid, and go from there. If fear is the problem, you will find many tips for dealing with fear in chapter eight. Usually, more time and energy are spent feeling bad about not doing the task than it takes to complete it. The most important tip to remember is to take one step; even the smallest baby step in the right direction will move you forward.

It has been noted by researchers that the greater number of times you do something and succeed, the longer your brain stores the information that helped you succeed. Also, when you have a success, dopamine is released in your brain and it is responsible for motivation, pleasure and learning. That is why breaking down your steps to small achievable ones will help you succeed even more.

PLAN YOUR TIME

You've discovered what makes you happy. You've created your goals and broken them down into achievable tasks. You've started working on some of the tasks and you're working on completing your unfinished business. So, now you have a better idea about what you need to do to get things done, and what is realistic for your daily schedule. If you're like me, now that you know what you want to do, you may want to get it all done immediately, and you may feel frustrated that you are not seeing greater progress. Remember, slow and steady is the way to go. I often have to remind myself that this is the key to achieving any goal. You don't take one leap and get to the top of the Empire State Building. You walk up one step at a time. Sometimes, you may feel energetic and double up a step or two, but it's that steady process that gets you there. You can't even see the top for a long time, but you just keep climbing. Imagine if there were just ten more steps before you would get to the top and you turned around after all of that progress and never made it to the magnificent view. I know you can do this. Keep moving forward. The view will definitely be worth it!

Begin planning for tomorrow.
Do you want to have time each day to take your child to the park, work on the online course you are creating, write your book, exercise, edit your photos or search for your perfect job? Planning can help you keep moving. Planning is something that is really individual to you and your daily life. Take a few minutes to think about your daily responsibilities; don't forget what you learned about saying no, delegating, sharing and swapping when possible. Now it's time to read about the different ways you can organize your tasks and create a schedule that works for you to create the type of day you want to experience.

Complete the largest task first.
One way to plan is to list the number of tasks you decided you would work on each day and put the largest one first. This works well for two reasons: it allows you to work on the task that takes the most energy before you get too tired, and it creates an incredible feeling of accomplishment when you finish, which provides energy and makes the other tasks much easier to complete. When you save the more complicated task or the task you enjoy the least for last, it becomes much easier to put it off until another day, especially when you are tired. Once you decide to put off that task, the process is likely to continue until you have created one of those uncompleted tasks that suck the energy from you. So, don't let that happen. Try completing the largest task first, and you will see what I mean. The feeling is worth it!

Complete the greatest impact task first.
Remember the time-saving tip that you learned in the last chapter about giving priority to the most productive tasks? Another way to decide what to do first is to decide which task will have the most impact, whether it creates the most money, provides the most inspiration or gets you the closest to your major goal. This task, when done, will move you much closer to your goal and continue to motivate you to even greater productivity because you will move forward faster and feel accomplished after completing it.

Create a daily plan.
The *Daily Plan Worksheet* at the end of the chapter combines several of the methods already discussed into one planning process. When you use this process, you don't waste valuable working time trying to decide what to do. Using the small steps from the Action Plan and/or Mind Map you competed in Chapter 5 and recalling the number of activities you decided to complete each day, write the detailed tasks in the first column of the *Daily Plan Worksheet*, then fill in the estimated amount of time you think each activity will take to complete. Next, assign each activity a priority number from one to five, with the number one identifying the top priority and the number five identifying the lowest priority. Next, assign each activity an impact number, with the number one being the highest impact and the number five being the lowest impact. Leave the last column of the worksheet empty for now.

Once you have completed the first four columns, return to the worksheet and fill in the order of completion number in the last column by comparing columns two through four for each activity to determine which activities will benefit you the greatest and have the largest impact in the amount of time you have available. The first task or tasks you should complete are the tasks with the lowest numbers in the impact and priority column. For example, if a task takes a small amount of time, has a high priority and completing it will make a large impact, you will want to work on this first. If another task takes more time but has a high impact and high priority, you may want to do that next. Give the tasks that have low impact, low priority and take a lot of time a lower completion number. Once you know what order you will complete the tasks in, take action. It should not take long to transfer your daily number of tasks from your Action Plan Worksheet or Mind Map Worksheet and determine the completion order once you make this part of your routine. A good time to do this is when you are completing your daily review so you are ready to hit the ground running the following day. If are unable to get all the activities completed that day, place the uncompleted activities on your next day's worksheet and repeat the process.

Plan tasks, research and relax days.
Some people like to separate their week into planning days, task completion days and research days. They plan and research first then create a step-by-step list of tasks that they want to work on, and kick out one right after another all day long on the task days. You may want to try this process for a few days and see how it works for you and then re-evaluate. If what you are doing is working, keep walking up those steps! If it is not, keep experimenting with your planning process until you find what feels right for you and what creates the best outcomes. Don't forget to plan days to relax and enjoy yourself and your family too. You won't be productive if you're not energized.

DEVELOP A ROUTINE

Routines are important because consistent routines eventually turn into habits. I am usually working on many projects, and writing is more often than not one of my tasks. To make the best progress with writing, I have to feel refreshed. I have found that if I work on other tasks first, it is more difficult for me to go back to writing, and it takes me longer to produce the same amount of content. After discovering this and trying different schedules, I decided to start my writing first thing in the morning when I felt most rested. My routine consisted of a quick check of my email and a cup of hot tea after awakening, then I would make my bed, spread out all my materials on the bed, grab my computer that I charged the night before, fill my second cup of tea and start typing. Ironically, I usually get so focused on my writing that I never drink that second cup of tea, but it is part of my routine and it works! After spending a few hours writing, I feel accomplished and am ready to move on to the other tasks that I planned the night before. Before I started this routine, I tried sitting at the table, at a desk and on the couch, and after many trials, I found that the routine I just described worked best for me. Now, I don't even give it much thought. I grab my supplies and I'm on my way!

It may take a bit of trial and error to figure out what works for you, but after you explore several ways of doing something, you will soon discover the way that feels just right for you. Of course once you develop your routine, it is important to remain flexible. It is normal for situations to intervene, such as a sick child or a deadline. When this happens, just do what is necessary, don't get flustered, and as soon as you are able, return to your happy routine.

HOW GETTING ORGANIZED HELPS YOUR CHILD

Organization can be beneficial, and it can start at a very young age. I am not saying that everything has to be in order all the time, but lack of chaos at certain times is a good thing. For example, placing homework, and items for school in an organized place can make the day run smoother. Even young children can do this with direction the night before. Being organized when doing homework can cause fewer distractions. Helping children create fun ways to get organized can convey the benefits of organization in a fun way.

You can start very young by having your toddler color the outside of a folder. Inside, they can keep all their favorite drawings (after they have been proudly displayed on the wall or fridge for some time!). An older child could help build a wooden box, or go on a rummage sale hunt to find a cool box to store their sport equipment or technology in. Make it fun and it will work. Instead of saying things like, "What a mess you have" and "Why are your things always all over the place?" use creative ways to help your child get excited about organizing while sharing the benefits with them.

For little ones, explain that being organized and putting away toys right after they use them means they don't have to do it before bedtime, so it creates time to read an extra book before going to bed. When explaining this, select the example that would really matter to your child based on their likes and interests, for the greatest success. This can work for all ages. Being more organized will help your child while doing school work and everyday activities, such as locating needed items, getting places on time, and even handling complex situations, problem solving and writing.

Help your child clean up incompletes.
Cleaning up incomplete messes can help your child in several ways. When you clean up your incomplete messes, your child may notice a calmer more focused you. The clutter will be removed and if the clutter is physical, the decreased clutter may provide a more relaxed environment. If your child has several unfinished tasks, such as a project not done, a pile of sports equipment that they step over when they enter their room and that pile of cards on the kitchen table, helping your child plan ways to complete the tasks may benefit both of you. After your child completes the task, provide the appropriate praise and ask them how they feel now that it's done. Discuss your own experience cleaning or finishing a task you had put off, pointing out how the act of completing it took less time than the amount of time you stressed about it.

Help your child learn to plan.
Planning is important at every age. Planning and anticipating a fun day at the park or a play date with a friend can help a younger child know what to expect and get excited about an event. Reminding a child about an upcoming planned event they are looking forward to can also reinforce positive behavior. Planning can help an older child get organized and prepare for a task such as studying for finals or even going on vacation. If your child is preparing for finals, teach your child the benefits of reviewing all that has to be done and splitting the studying up into set time periods over an extended period of time versus not planning at all and finding out that time ran out before all the test subjects were reviewed.

Start planning with your child at a young age to develop this skill. Let your child help you plan a special day with family or a special meal. Have fun with it. Have your child write down the plan or even draw or cut out pictures about the planned event.

Help your child set the date, list the tasks that need to be done in advance and the times to complete them. Have fun with the details. If your child is helping you plan a special meal, help them consider many different things. Who will attend? What will be served? What groceries will need to be purchased? When will the shopping take place? Will you decorate the table? What order will the food be served? Have fun and don't forget to enjoy the event! Whenever you have the opportunity to have your child help you plan, include them. This will help provide many different planning experiences.

For an older child who may be struggling with a difficult future plan, share some of the tips you have learned, such as prioritizing tasks and splitting up the tasks into research and task days if appropriate. The tips may also be very beneficial when working on school projects and practicing for something that is important to them. It could even help a child who wants to improve in a sport or excel at playing an instrument. Planning skills will greatly benefit your child when they leave the nest, attend college and get their first job.

Create routines for your child.
It has been written in research time and time again that routines greatly benefit children. Starting in infancy, routines are known to build trust that will be used for years to come, because when a child is part of a routine, the child will begin to learn what to expect next. Routines teach babies and toddlers self-control and provide comfort and a sense of safety, since they can anticipate what will happen next. This can help them feel secure, learn trust and provide emotional stability. Routines can also reduce power struggles, develop social skills, help with transitions and help parents adjust to parenthood. So yes, routines are important for sure! That is exactly why a consistent bedtime routine can greatly help a child go to sleep at night; it can also decrease those bedtime tantrums and benefit the parent. Your child will know what to expect and will be mentally prepared as they go through the same consistent steps each night before going to bed. It doesn't mean there won't be resistance at times, but consistent

routines will greatly reduce it. Consistency in dealing with the resistance is key. Once a child discovers that if they resist long enough they will get their way, it only reinforces the message to continue the tantrum even longer to get what they want, and it intensifies the problem instead of correcting it.

Routines can help an older child decrease stress and feel more organized. Routines can take away the need and time required for additional planning. When your child knows what is coming next, they have time to mentally prepare for it and to adjust much more easily. If an older child has a routine that consists of practicing their trumpet each evening, they do not have to try to find the time to fit in practice, and they will know they will arrive at music class prepared. This can create less anxiety on music class days, prevent anxiety or a bad mood, and create a sense of accomplishment for being prepared. The results of using this routine can actually impact the entire family in a positive way.

GET ORGANIZED REVIEW

1. Freeing your mind of the feelings that go along with an unfinished task can allow you to direct more energy toward other productive tasks.

2. Planning can help you keep moving. Slow and steady will get you to your goals. You may not see the end result at first, but remember not to turn around when you're almost there.

3. Planning is something that is individual to you and your daily life. Consider your daily responsibilities and don't forget about saying no, delegating, sharing and swapping when possible.

4. There are many ways to plan, including planning the night before and putting tasks at the top of the list that are the largest, will have the most impact, will create the most money, or will get you the closest to your major goal.

5. Feeling accomplished with an early task will motivate you and make it easier to complete additional tasks.

6. Routines become habits, helping you reach your goals.

7. Experimenting with different techniques will help you find what works best for you.

8. Flexibility is important.

Get Organized Exercises

1. Complete the *Unfinished Business Worksheet*. Walk through your house and look for unfinished tasks. If they can be done in a short time, complete them. If not, schedule a time to complete them or have someone else complete them. This can decrease your stress and free up energy to use on other tasks.

2. Plan for the following day, while taking into consideration your daily commitments.

3. Delegate, swap, share or eliminate tasks when it is beneficial to you.

4. Complete the *Daily Plan Worksheet* by following the instructions and documenting the estimated time, priority level, and impact level of your daily tasks. Consider the largest task, the highest impact task, the task with the highest potential to earn money or the task that gets you closest to your larger goal, as you plan and complete your worksheet. Then, determine which order works best to motivate you.

5. Continue to conduct your Daily Review at the end of each day, using the work sheet from the previous chapter. Continue to adjust your Daily Plan as needed.

6. Do this for several days until you establish the right process that works for your schedule and personality.

7. Maintain this new routine until it becomes a habit.

8. Feel grateful that by creating organization in your life, both you and your child will benefit.

Get Organized Exercises to Help Your Child

1. Create a sense of organization at a very young age. I am not saying everything should be in order all the time, but lack of chaos at certain times, such as heading out the door for school, is a good thing.

2. Use creative ways to get your child excited about organizing while sharing the benefits with them. For example, let your toddler color on the outside of a folder to keep drawings in and help an older child build a box to store sport equipment in.

3. Start planning with your child at a young age to develop this skill. Let your child help you plan a special day with family or a special meal.

4. For an older child who may be struggling with a difficult future plan, share some of the tips you have learned such as prioritizing tasks and splitting up the tasks into research and task days if appropriate.

5. Create an organized environment and a system to decrease distraction when completing school work and with everyday activities, such as locating items, getting places on time, handling complex situations, problem solving and writing.

6. Establish routines starting in infancy. Routines build trust, increase self-control, provide comfort and a sense of safety, reduce power struggles, develop social skills, help with transitions and help parents adjust to parenthood.

UNFINISHED BUSINESS WORKSHEET

Make a list of all of the tasks you constantly put off doing and the messes you walk past every day. Schedule a date to complete each one. Tackling unfinished business will increase your ability to achieve and will provide you with a calming sense of clarity.

Unfinished Task/Mess	Scheduled date of completion	Completed? YES/NO
Example: Clean entranceway to the house and put all boots, coats and papers away.	Today	YES!
Example: Return empty bottles	This Saturday	

Now that you have documented your unfinished business, go back until you have written YES in every column.
YOU are now ready to focus all your energy on

YOUR IDEAL LIFE!

DAILY PLAN WORKSHEET

Date_____

Use the Time, Priority and Impact columns to determine the most productive use of your available time. For example, if an activity requires a small amount of time, is a top priority and will have a large impact on how quickly you will achieve your goal, do this first. If you can weave the activities that take less time into convenient places, such as waiting at dance class or during your lunch break, this will stretch your time.

Activity	Estimated Time in Minutes	Priority level High=1 Low=5	Impact Level High=1 Low=5	Order of Completion
Hire designer for business logo	10 minutes	1 **2** 3 4 5	**1** 2 3 4 5	1
Listen to podcast about motivation	30 minutes	1 2 3 **4** 5	1 2 **3** 4 5	2

Now that you have documented the time estimate, impact and priority level, go back and fill in the order of completion for each task, but don't forget to remain flexible as the day evolves so you can complete as much as possible and reach your goals!

CHAPTER 8

CONQUER FEAR!

I promised we would talk about fear. If you've completed the chapter exercises so far, you may already be experiencing it. Fear can be paralyzing, but it doesn't have to be.

When I was eight years old I took my first plane ride. My aunt purchased a ticket for me to visit her in Virginia. I went all by myself. It was a beautifully sunny day. My mother made sure I was safely on the plane for the 45-minute ride, and my aunt was already waiting at the Washington DC airport to pick me up. I was excited as I climbed the steps to the plane in my brand-new pink and green flowered sundress. The stewardess walked me to my seat and made sure I was comfortable and not afraid. She showed me where the call button was located in case I needed her, and before I knew it, I was in the air.

Not long after takeoff, a young man got up from his seat and started to walk to the front of the plane. I vividly remember how tall and muscular he was. He didn't have hair on his head and it was very shiny. I had never seen a young man who was bald. I had only seen bald heads on older men, like my grandfather, and he still had a bit of fuzzy hair near his ears. I remembered a show I once saw on TV about a man who highjacked a plane, and as I watched the young man walk toward the front of the plane, I realized there was a hijacker on our plane. I sat there in frozen silence as I saw him open a closed door and enter into an area in the front of the plane. There had been stories in the news about hijackers diverting planes to other places. I worried about how I would get back to Washington DC if he flew the plane somewhere else. Then I thought about how worried my mother and aunt would be. I considered whether I would be in danger if I put my call light on to alert the stewardess, who must not have been paying close enough attention to her passengers, as she should have been! The three minutes he was out of sight seemed like an eternity. The entire time I held my shaking finger one inch above the call button and my stomach was in knots. I finally decided to press the call button just as the man came back through the door. I sat frozen, terrified because he was coming my way. The man was walking towards me, and I began to panic.

Then, at that exact moment I thought I might throw up, he smiled at me and sat back down in his seat. Just then, the stewardess came up to me while pointing to the door the man came out of and asked me if I wanted to use the restroom. She said she would walk me there. I followed her to the restroom and luckily, I had not wet my seat! After what seemed like hours of intense fear, I realized I mistakenly imagined the entire situation. I checked out the cool restroom and once back in my seat, I started to giggle and enjoyed the rest of the flight. I had fun looking for animals in the clouds, just like I used to do lying on my back in my yard, and then before I knew it, we landed in Washington DC. What an adventure my first plane ride was! Over the years, my plane ride story has been retold many times by family, and it is always followed by lots of laughter.

My plane ride memory is a great example of how you can perceive fear in your mind that can feel so real, your body physically reacts. My hands were shaking, my stomach was churning and what was really happening was as simple as this: I was on a short plane ride with other people and one young gentleman had to use the restroom. That's it! I'm sure you can think of similar examples where you experienced a physical reaction to an imagined fear. Maybe your mind created fear when you were expecting someone to arrive at a certain time on a snowy day and they were late, or maybe you imagined something bad would happen when you performed in your school play or talent show. Maybe you are creating fear right now as you think about asking your boss for a raise, or preparing to let your child spend the night away from home for the first time. It happens more than you realize, and it happens more to some people than others. The difference between highly successful people and others is that the highly successful people don't let, or no longer let, fear stop them.

FEAR DISOLVERS

There are many things you can do to dissolve your fears. The tips may not always get rid of your fears completely, but they may melt them down to something that is manageable and will not stop you from taking action and moving forward. Try each fear dissolver tip with the current fears you are facing, and then you will find the ones that work best for you. Don't let fear stop you!

You are a busy person and have no time for fear, so let's hit it head on. You found out what makes you happy. You are practicing positivity and noticing how good it makes you feel. Others have noticed the changes too. You broke down your goals, selected the number you want to focus on each day and scheduled time in your day to work on those goals. You cleared up some of the tasks you had left unfinished and established a routine that works for you. You are all set to start, maybe you have even checked off some of your small goal-related tasks, and now here comes Mr. Fear. There are several reasons why you develop fear, but you will soon find out that fear can also be your friend.

Fear may start as you begin to doubt and think things like, "Why am I trying to do this?" "It's hard," "I will never have time to do this," "It will take me years." Mr. Fear sneaks up on you and you start to think things like, "What if I fail?" "What if I tell people and they laugh?" "What if my friends or family judge me for wanting to start my own business when my children are so young?"

What you need to know is that fear is two things. It can be helpful and it is often a normal part of the success process. Think about it this way, if you don't experience any fear at all, then it could be that your goal is way too small! Maybe you haven't stretched yourself as far as you're able. Maybe you are not moving forward at all.

Experiencing fear, even a perceived fear, produces changes in the brain's fear center, called the amygdala. Fear can also heighten your awareness and cause bodily reactions such as heart acceleration, faster breathing or increased perspiration in less than one second after you experience it. You are not just imagining the physical response from perceived fear; you are creating it.

When you are able to bypass your fear, the feeling is tremendous. Don't let perceived fears stand in your way. Do your research and move forward. Ask anyone who has a successful business or who has had a large achievement if they ever experienced fear along the way, and if they tell you no, I'd bet they aren't being completely truthful. I'm here to say you will experience fear, you will experience obstacles and you will have to quiet your self-talk from time to time, but that is all part of the process of growth. If you experience fear, you are moving in the right direction. I am here to show you ways to calm your fears.

Replace your fear.
One of the known methods for dealing with fear is to replace the fearful thought with a pleasant thought. The conditioned response doesn't erase the original fear, but it leads to a new, safer thought. For example, if you feared flying on a plane but had to fly if you wanted to visit your new grandchild in Australia, instead of focusing on the flight, focus on the images of holding your beloved grandbaby in your arms. Imagine the warmth, the smell and the feeling you get when he looks into your eyes. You will begin to relax and feel a bit calmer if you do this throughout your trip.

Explore your fear.
One way to dissolve a fear is to explore it and then imagine the positive outcome you will receive once you face it head on. One trick that always works for me is thinking about what is making me fearful and then trying to understand it.

You can do this too, by asking yourself three questions:

1. What am I afraid to do?
2. What is the scary outcome I imagine would happen?
3. What is something good that could happen if I do it despite my fear?

Here's example #1

What am I afraid to do?
I am afraid to call the person I would like to have as my mentor and ask him if he would like to mentor me.

What is the scary outcome I imagine would happen?
The person would be rude to me, laugh at me or not want to be my mentor, and I would feel embarrassed.

What is something good that could happen if I do it despite my fear?
The person agrees to be my mentor or they decline explaining they are very busy, but suggest another mentor who would be a much better fit.

Example #2

What am I afraid to do?
I'm afraid to present to a group.

What is the scary outcome I imagine would happen?
I will make a mistake and everyone will laugh at me, think I'm not intelligent and think I do not know what I am talking about.

What is something good that could happen if I do it despite my fear?

I present even though I'm frightened. I do a great job and some of the people come up to me after my talk and want to buy my product, write about my product, put me on their podcast, ask me to write a blog for them, and ask me to talk at their event, etc.

Instead of focusing on your fear (Question #1), focus on the positive outcome (Question #3). Feeling embarrassed is something that you create yourself. Your thoughts create your feelings. It's all about negative self-talk, so don't even go there.

Your negative self-talk is hijacking your common sense! Instead, focus on the positive result. If you do not get your intended result, that is ok. Try to see any way you still can benefit. For instance, in the fear example about asking someone to be a mentor, if you are told no, try to obtain information or make connections that may help you if possible, then move on to your next person. Don't sweat the small stuff.

List your fears.
It is time to make a list of the fears that are preventing you from moving forward. Using the *Overcome Your Fear Worksheet* at the end of the chapter, create your list and ask yourself the three questions listed on the worksheet and focus on the great outcomes. Visualize the outcomes in your head, psych yourself up and take action! Don't forget to use the *Victory List Worksheet* you completed in chapter four to help build yourself up and increase your confidence before you face Mr. Fear, and remember, he's really not such a bad guy after all.

One day, I was working as a consultant online and I had another project that I also wanted to work on. I couldn't work fewer hours on my online job because I depended on the income, but I really wanted to create more time to take on the other project. After brainstorming all my options, I decided the best way to make it work would be to ask to work fewer hours for the same pay at my online job, which was technically a raise. So, not only would I make more money per hour, but I would be devoting less time to the project. The thought of making this request made me shudder. I had never done anything like that before. I evaluated my fear and discovered that my main fear was that I would be laughed at and maybe lose the contract I already had. "You want to work fewer hours for the same pay?" I imagined my boss saying. Then I asked myself what good could happen if I asked, despite my fear? I realized I would most likely not lose my contract, and all I was really worried about was feeling embarrassed if I was told no. I changed my self-talk and thought of all the reasons why I should be told yes, including how hard I worked, and how many additional hours I worked in the past without pay. I continued brainstorming reasons until I felt more confident, and then I scheduled the meeting to make my request. I asked the question and did not even have to explain why I was requesting before I received the answer that I wanted to hear. That additional time allowed me to work on a project that propelled my career forward, causing my life to take a wonderful turn. Now each time a similar fear arises, I look back at the many benefits I received from facing that one fear, and I know that I have to keep facing my fears to succeed.

Look back at your fearprints.
That leads me right to the next fear dissolver that I call fearprints. Fearprints are much like footprints. They are imprints of fearful experiences encountered in the past that have been successfully conquered while moving toward a goal. For example, I do not like to fly long distances in airplanes, but many years ago, I summoned the courage to take my first trip to Italy despite my fear. Whenever I get that same fearful feeling as I contemplate flying, I remind myself about the positive outcome that resulted in a fun and memorable trip that I was able to make because I confronted that fear.

Take the time to fill out the *Follow Your Fearprints Worksheet* at the end of the chapter. Document past fears that you have faced successfully, the positive results that followed when you faced those fears, and the lesson you took away from the experience. Read the example below to understand how to fill out the worksheet. After completing this exercise, use this worksheet along with the *Victory List Worksheet* you created in chapter four, every time you are about to face a fear or need to feel more confident.

Example

I was afraid to try out for the school talent show.

Benefits

I was in the show. I felt proud in front of my parents and classmates. I didn't mess up. I felt more confident afterwards. I was asked to join a band. I became a better guitar player. I made new friends that I am still in touch with today.

Lesson Learned
It is natural to feel fear before doing something in front of others, but the benefits that I received from doing it were worth the small fear I faced.

Use your fear-magination
Another way to face your fears is to imagine away the fear. I had a friend who was going to a small business dinner and found out that one of the guests was her old boss who once tried unsuccessfully to fire her. My friend quit that job because she felt she was being treated unfairly. She had found a job at her present company. She was really worried about how the dinner would go and what this woman might say to her present boss. Her present employer did not know her connection to her ex-boss and she feared this woman still held a grudge. As much as she wanted to, there was no way to get out of the meeting. She wanted everything to go smoothly. She told me that when she thought about the meeting, she got so nervous, her hands would start shaking and she felt like she was going to hyperventilate. She decided that each time she got nervous in the days before the event, she would take a few minutes and visualize a highly successful meeting. She visualized what people were wearing, how professional they were, where they were sitting, the topics of conversation and even the smell and taste of the food. She visualized a really relaxing fun successful dinner meeting, and it helped her feel less tense. The day after the dinner meeting, she called and sounded so excited. She said she was shocked at how close her visualization matched the actual meeting, right down to where everyone was seated. She said that as soon as the event started, she felt relaxed and confident that the dinner meeting was going to be a great success. This method is actually a way to practice an event before it even happens. Athletes, performers and speakers often use this method as they prepare for important events.

Expose your fear.
Another way to dissolve fear is to see how you can decrease the potential risk or fear by blasting it into smaller parts. This is

similar to what therapists describe as exposure therapy, which is exposure to the feared activities, situations and objects in a safe environment. For example, if you are afraid to give a speech in front of a large group, try first to talk in front of one person you trust, then invite a few friends to listen to you, then maybe a small group at your church or place of business, then as you feel more confident and prepared, review the lists that you made of your victories and your fearprints and then go for it! Remember to also think about the benefits you can receive from facing the fear and how it may even lead to something that can be life changing!

Sample it and get feedback.
Another way to help dissolve your fear is to start with a smaller sample and get feedback to guide you. For example, if you wanted to work from home and sell a product online but are not sure if you will be able to sell your product and you don't want to get stuck with a garage full of it, start small. You could even start by interviewing a few people from your intended market first, then if all goes well, give out one or two products and get feedback. After that, try to sell one, then two and so on. You will also learn more and develop increased confidence along the way.

Another example would be if you were afraid to make sales calls but had to begin making them as part of your new job assignment. You could first try to call someone you didn't really care if you sold your product to for practice. That way, you would greatly decrease your disappointment if the sale didn't happen. Make sure that it is someone in your niche so you can truly test your pitch. Then, if you make the sale, that is great, but if you don't, you will not be disappointed and you will also have gained experience. People who want practice and are trying to refine their technique without losing the big sale often use this technique. Do not be afraid to ask if they would be willing to help you by sharing their thoughts on your product and message. You may be surprised how much it can help you if they provide honest feedback. Sampling fear can really benefit you.

Do it anyway.
One other way to handle fear is to simply ignore the fear and just do it. Did you ever jump off a high diving board at a pool? Do you remember the first time you did it? I do. I had so much fear in the pit of my stomach, but there was no turning back. Other kids were in line, and I knew I had to go. I ran as fast as I could and held my breath as I went off the edge. I was afraid but did it anyway.

If there is something you really want badly and you are willing to take the risks that go along with the potential outcome, then just do it and don't let anything stop you. Educate yourself about the topic or process; consider all the consequences and how you would address them if they happened. Don't forget to consider the great potential outcomes, then feel the fear and go for it. I really don't enjoy flying, but I do it anyway. Each time I fly, I remind myself about the enormous number of successful flights around the world every day, and I focus on the exciting things I will do once I get to the destination, I can face my fears. I can't imagine the wonderful experiences I would not have had, such as visiting the Coliseum in Rome, the rainforest in Panama and the beautiful walks down the Thames River, if I had given into my fear.

Tally your fears.
A fun method of approaching your fears is by playing the Tally Your Fear game. This activity makes facing fears a bit more fun by creating a game out of facing your daily fears. You play the game by keeping a tally of how many fears you face each day along with the outcomes. Some people try to face one or two fears a day, just to experience continued growth, while others face even more. They don't have to be large, scary fears, but just enough to get you moving and to build your confidence for the higher challenges that may come your way. I was recording my daily tally in a notebook at first, but then I decided to purchase a fear journal. The journal includes helpful quotes related to fear and helps me focus on the fears I have faced successfully. It reminds me that most of the fear is made up in my mind and the

benefits I achieve due to facing my fears would never have been realized if I had given into the fear.

Start by doing one thing you fear each day. Once you successfully move past that fear, add another and another. The fears do not all have to be large fears like speaking to a crowd of thousands or jumping from a plane. They can include things you would like to be more comfortable doing no matter how small they may be, such as turning down a request, making better eye contact when you talk, or inviting a neighbor over. Last Monday, I faced six small fears head on and five had successful outcomes. Not a bad percentage! Keep a tally each day of the number of fears you faced and the number that were successful. Record those numbers in a notebook or journal. You can even expand this concept further by tallying up your daily numbers into a running tally for each month, then each year. It will be eye opening to see the number of times you successfully faced your fears and the limited number of times your outcome was not a success. When you start seeing that you are successfully conquering a large percentage of your fears, you will find it easier to face more or even larger fears because you will know that the odds are in your favor that you will have a great outcome! Use your *Victory List Worksheet, Follow Your Fearprints Worksheet* and your running tally score to build up your confidence before you take future steps that scare you, such as making a difficult phone call or speaking in public.

Steer the fear.
Another successful method to use when facing your fears is to do what I call, "steer the fear." By preparing for the fear you believe may happen, you can easily steer the situation without panic. For example, if you think someone will question how you have the expertise to do something, have a list of your qualifications written on a bio sheet or practice how you would naturally and politely answer the question to convince the person asking the question, why you are the perfect person to take this on. This is a good tactic if you are ever going to be interviewed by the media.

It helped me once when I was getting a critique at a writer's conference. I feared that I would be questioned about why a book I wrote about child development wasn't better suited to have been written by a physician. I practiced my answer to this question by myself first and then I role played with a friend. I created a one-page bio that listed all my qualifications. I was ready and confident that if I was asked that question, I would be able to answer without skipping a beat. When I walked in the room I was a bit nervous, but I was also feeling confident and excited that this was my chance to shine. Once introductions were complete, we got straight to business and the question I feared was the very first question I was asked. If I had not prepared, I would have stumbled, been embarrassed and then spent the rest of the meeting replaying what I *should* have said in my head. But since I was prepared, I took a breath and confidently explained why I was the perfect person to write the book, while simultaneously sliding my prepared bio across the table. The Critic nodded and I didn't even have to finish my speech before he agreed that my years of professional experience made me the perfect candidate to write a book on this topic of development. In this case, the thing that I feared the most was actually a great thing to happen to me, because it provided the perfect opportunity for me to expand a bit about my past experience by going into much greater detail than I would have felt comfortable doing on my own.

Commit and submit.
One more way to face your fears is to make a commitment to take the challenge, but don't get so attached to the perfect results. Sometimes, it helps to face a fear by just casually giving it a try. Just do it and don't put too much emphasis on the results. Submit to the fact that you don't have to like the outcome. For example, if you want to ask someone to mentor you, just make the call, but before you do, tell yourself that it's not a big deal if this person says no, because there are many other people who could help and you could actually end up with someone who is even a better fit for you if this first person says no. You may

think, "Sure, it would be fantastic if this person would mentor me, but if not, it is not the end of the world." If the person says no, it may create an obstacle for you and you may have to rethink your plan a bit or find a different way around the obstacle, but it is not a showstopper. It is not the end of the world, and you can still reach your goal. Often, when you look at obstacles you have experienced throughout your life, you will find many times when things like this happen and many times you may not have even realized it at the time until you look back on the situation at a later date. So remember, you have already navigated around many obstacles and you will continue to successfully do so.

HOW CONQUERING FEAR HELPS YOUR CHILD

Everyone has fears throughout life, and if you look back at your childhood, you will probably remember some things you were afraid of. Maybe it was meeting new classmates on your first day of school, giving that dreaded report in front of the class, or it might even have been that monster you were sure hung out under your bed at night. For me, it was the pink and white giraffe clothes rack in my bedroom that I hung my robe and clothes on. It was a friendly tall spotted giraffe that I loved to look at during the day, but once the day ended and nightfall came, it terrified me! The clothes rack appeared to turn into a big scary man at night when it was basked in the moonlight peaking in through the window. Help your child conquer their fears and let your child see you conquering your own. Once your child observes you conquering your fears or hears your success stories, they will learn two things. They will learn that other people, including moms, have fears, and they will learn fears can be successfully conquered.

Many of the techniques in this chapter can help children of all ages combat their fears. Use the tips in this chapter to help your child work through fears. Because there are many tips in this chapter, you may want to return to this chapter when you or your child face a significant fear to review and find the tips that would work the best in that particular situation. Below, you will find examples of how some of the tips may help your child in situations that your child may experience.

Explore the fear with your child.
The giraffe fear could have been easily resolved by the knowledge that when clothes are draped over the giraffe, it changed the shape of the rack. Then when the light shined in from the window, it caused a shadow to appear, making the stand look much bigger! One fun way to help resolve a similar fear is to use a flashlight and create fun puppet shadows on the wall while telling fun stories so the child can see how the light can reflect into different shadows that look larger and resemble other things. By creating finger shadows, the child gets to sample the fear and try to understand what is behind it. Another fun way to do this for a bit older child may be taking a trip to the library to get a book about making shadow puppets. Reading a science book about how shadows are created could help an older child understand the concept, have fun and become more knowledgeable at the same time. Once the fear is identified, in this scenario, it could be left up to the child whether to move the giraffe so the light can't hit it anymore or leave it in place so the cool shadow, which is much larger than they can make with their fingers, is created on their bedroom wall at night. After the fun shadow activities are complete and your child understands a bit more about the science behind it, you might be surprised at the answer you receive!

Many times, it may be beneficial to combine several of the tips in the chapter when helping your child deal with a fear. I will describe the situation followed by several ways to apply the tips from the chapter. Let's say your child was given the assignment to present an oral report to their class. They have come to you and are very fearful of doing this. Please keep reading to see the tips I selected from the chapter and ideas of ways to apply them to this situation.

Teach your child how to replace the fear.
Show your child how to replace the fear of speaking in front of their class with a positive outcome, just like you did when you

filled out the *Overcome Your Fear Worksheet*. You may have to help your child brainstorm the positives that could happen to help them understand the concept and get them started. They may even come up with a few you haven't considered.

Help your child explore the fear.
Identifying and discussing the fears with a parent can be helpful. Remember to discuss the following three questions with your child.

1. What are they afraid to do?
2. What is the scary outcome they imagine would happen?
3. What is something good that could happen if they do it despite their fear?

Once your child identifies the fear, they may want to watch a short video or book about presenting to a group or about overcoming fear. If your child is younger, you can help them select the book or video to ensure it is appropriate for their age level and situation.

Have your child look back at fearprints.
Explain to your child that everyone faces fears whether big or small, every day. Point out some of the fears that your child has overcome and ask your child to also brainstorm situations related to their fear of speaking in public, where they faced fear in the past and how they succeeded. You can also expand upon the topic of overcoming fear and discuss any fears they have successfully faced in the past.

Show your child how to use fear-magination.
As a child gets older, you can use an example from their childhood, such as the fear of a monster hiding under a bed, to explain the concept of how often fear is something we perceive in our own minds. Talk to your child about visualizing the outcome they want to achieve. Explain to them that many famous athletes and performers have successfully used this technique. Guide them as they first tell you exactly how they

want their presentation experience to go, and then have them close their eyes and visualize it. Ask them to use all their senses and practice visualization many times before they present.

Teach your child how to sample the fear.
Suggest to your child that they slowly sample the fear by tackling small pieces of it one at a time. You could suggest first practicing their speech in the mirror, then in front of a parent, and then in front of a few friends before they present to the whole class.

Help your child steer the fear.
Help your child brainstorm and prepare for what to do if something doesn't go as planned. Preparing a handout or a visual to use during the presentation, if allowed, may also be helpful because it may help guide their presentation, add to the value of their presentation, and distract their nervousness a bit while decreasing the direct attention focused solely on them.

While those are just a few of the actions you can take to help your child face the fear of speaking in public, the important message is, there are many ways to teach your child techniques to decrease fear so they can move forward in life.

Just remember, while using all the tips in this chapter, as age allows, explain what fear is and how using the specific "tricks" you are suggesting to your child can help them no matter what age they are, even into adulthood. Explain that it is natural to have some fears at any age and that everyone has them.

When explaining fear to your child, do not forget to mention the important message that sometimes fear is good because fear helps us by alerting us to something that can be dangerous. Let your child know that if they ever feel that they or anyone else will be harmed or is in any potential danger, always immediately tell an adult and never face that fear alone.

One last fun way to teach your child about overcoming fear is to play the Tally the Fear game with your child. You can also ask your child to think of the small fears that they experienced that particular day, how they successfully faced those fears, as well as any fears they had that they did not successfully face. You can also share your own. This can even be a dinner table discussion. This is a great way to see the challenges your child is facing every day, to help them gain confidence and to remind them of their achievements for when they face a larger challenge in the future.

CONQUER FEAR CHAPTER REVIEW

1. Fear is normal and can be part of the process of moving forward.
2. Your body reacts physically to fear that you create in your mind.
3. Fear can be paralyzing if you let it. Don't let it!
4. Highly successful people don't let perceived fear stop them from taking action.
5. Fear dissolvers are techniques to decrease your fear. Although they may not get rid of your fears completely, they may melt them down to fears that become manageable and will not stop you from taking action and moving forward.

    Fear dissolvers include:

    - Replacing the perceived outcome with a positive outcome.
    - Exploring your fear by asking the following questions:
        1. What am I afraid to do?
        2. What is the scary outcome I imagine would happen?
        3. What is something good that could happen if I do it despite my fear?
    - Reminding yourself of your fearprints, which are past fears you've successfully overcome.
    - Using your fear-magination by visualizing a positive outcome using all of your senses.
    - Breaking down your fear and slowly exposing yourself to it to decrease your perceived risk.
    - Sampling your fear by practicing and testing and getting feedback.

- Educating yourself after considering all outcomes, then do it anyway.
- Playing the Tally the Fear game by keeping track of the number of daily fears encountered and the number successfully conquered each day, to practice facing small fears every day and to reinforce your ability to conquer fears.
- Steering your fear by preparing and practicing for the feared outcomes in advance.
- Taking a step back; not getting attached to just one outcome and just doing it.
- Weighing your fears vs. your dreams and ignoring the fear and doing it anyway.

Conquer Fear Exercises

1. Make a list of your fears using the *Overcome Your Fear Worksheet*, answer the three questions, then focus on the positive outcomes.
2. Make a list of your fearprints using the *Follow Your Fearprints Worksheet*. Include fears you successfully challenged, the positive results you achieved and the lesson you learned. Review this and your *Victory List Worksheet* from chapter four whenever you need extra encouragement.
3. Practice using the fear dissolvers explained in the chapter and listed in the chapter review to find the ones that work the best for you and for each particular situation.
4. Play the Tally Your Fear game.
5. Feel grateful that by facing the fears in your life, both you and your child will benefit.

Conquer Fear Exercises to Help Your Child

1. Let your child know that it is natural to have some worries or fears, and that everyone has them.

2. When your child is afraid to do something, ask your child the three questions in this chapter.

    - What are they afraid to do?
    - What is the scary outcome they imagine would happen?
    - What is something good that could happen if they do it despite their fear?

3. Once your child's perceived fear is identified, introduce the appropriate fear dissolvers in this chapter, depending on your child's development and understanding.

4. Explain to your child that at times, fear can be good, because it can alert us to situations that can be dangerous. Let your child know that if they ever feel that they or anyone else will be harmed or could be in danger, they should always immediately tell an adult and never face that fear alone.

5. Play the Tally Your Fear game with your child.

OVERCOME YOUR FEAR WORKSHEET

Fear can be powerful but is often imagined and not real. List the fears that have stopped you from moving forward by answering the questions on this worksheet.

What am I afraid to do?	What is the scary outcome I imagine would happen?	What good could happen if I do it despite my fear?
Example: I am afraid to ask someone to mentor me.	They would be rude, laugh, and refuse. I would feel embarrassed.	The person agrees or declines politely explaining they are busy, and they suggest another mentor.

Now that you have documented your fears, focus on the last column and imagine the good that will happen. By doing this, you will eliminate your negative imagined results, so you can

CRUSH YOUR FEARS!

FOLLOW YOUR FEARPRINTS WORKSHEET

Often, fears are imagined and not real. Make a list of the past fears that you challenged and successfully overcame. Include the positive results you received by facing your fears.

Leave the last column empty for now.

Past Fear	Positive Result	Lesson Learned
Example: I was afraid to try out for the school talent show.	I made it. I felt proud in front of my parents/classmates. I didn't mess up. I felt confident. I was asked to join a band. I became a better guitarist. I made friends that I am still in touch with today.	It is natural to feel fear before doing something in front of others, but the benefits that I received from doing it were worth the small fear I faced.

Return to the last column and include the lessons you learned when you challenged your imagined fears. Return to this list often as you follow your fearprints and

CRUSH FUTURE FEARS!

CHAPTER 9

LEARN TO LOVE LEARNING

It used to be that one of the only ways to get an education was to go to school, and that caused problems when there was not time or money to do so, or if a person did not excel in classroom-style learning. Today, there are many ways to learn. Just about anyone, regardless of income, time constraints or learning difficulties, can find a way to become an expert in any field they choose.

You may be asking yourself, "How can I reach my goals when there is so much I still need to learn to do before I can even begin?" Well, I'm here to tell you that you do not always need to know how to do everything when you start. You can learn as you go. That is the beauty of it. Learning as a method of achieving your goals is nothing like traditional school, because you get to choose all your topics and the method you want to use to obtain the information.

When I decided to become an entrepreneur, I did not know how to use social media at all. I had never published a book. I didn't have hands-on experience with marketing. I had never listened to a podcast and did not know about freelancing. I am happy to say that while working a fulltime job and raising a family, I became proficient in areas I never even knew existed. I had fun building up my knowledge base. I am amazed at how conducive the Internet is to learning about any topic you may ever consider! You can read about the latest research, watch how-to videos, get motivated from others, connect with people and find the greatest resources in the world. You can even contact some of the major experts in just about any field. You can do this all without leaving your home. I now commit many satisfying hours to continual learning and achieving my dreams, and you can too!

SMART HACKS

Technology is your friend whether you are comfortable using it or not. You don't have to know everything. The information is there if you need it. With technology, you have 24-hour access to online courses, free information, freelancers, university research, language programs, statistics, a thesaurus and just about anything else you would ever want to know. The days of heading off to the library, taking in-person classes, attending weeklong trainings, searching through large research manuals and traveling to the experts can now be over if you want them to be. Today, information can be with you constantly. This is something to take advantage of whenever you can and in any quantity that fits your lifestyle and schedule. If you were able to attend college or even get your PhD, that's great and the experience that took you along that path will be with you forever, but as technology expands, it is very possible to become an expert on any topic you decide to pursue, without interrupting your life. It is possible to fit it into your own unique schedule and connect with experts along the way.

Here is one example of how I personally continued to learn while I was working a full-time job. I would start the day listening to a short audio on my computer as I prepared for the day. My drive to work was just the right length of time to listen to an inspiring podcast interview of thriving entrepreneurs and the successes they had achieved. This was both motivational and informative. It never failed that I would end up learning a cool hack to use for marketing, social media or other cool methods to advance my business, while also getting psyched about my plan. Several times a week I used part of my lunch hour to get exercise and sunshine while walking and listening to training webinars on many different topics. Other times, I joined in on live training calls.

Even now, every other Saturday, I wake up an hour early to join in a one-hour mastermind call. I will explain more about mastermind groups in chapter ten.

While traveling on longer trips, I listen to audios that teach me about new topics or motivate me to achieve. My husband has now joined me in doing this. While waiting for dental or other appointments, I read the many tutorial books that I have downloaded for free on my phone. A few times a year, I plan a day to attend a workshop or training or attend local meeting groups. And those are just some of the ways I continually learn.

As a busy parent, you can decide which of the following smart hacks below work for you and your schedule. But even if only one of them fits your daily routine, you will still be on your way to greatly expanding your knowledge and successfully reaching your dreams.

Take advantage of information overload.
If you perform an online search for topics such as marketing, social media, parenting, weight loss, leadership skills or just about any topic, you will find all kinds of information from very reputable sources. Often, you will find offers to download free information or eBooks or to watch webinars and videos about the topics that interest you. Take advantage of it, and the next time you are waiting for an appointment, learn something new!

Find perma-free books.
One way to obtain free information is to look in the business or self-help areas on some of the major book sites such as Amazon. Often, there are eBooks listed there that are listed as perma-free, which means they are permanently free. You can usually get enough information from the free books to get started, and at times, you can also find very detailed books this way. For example, I did a search on Amazon using the words "free books," and the results pulled up over 91,000 eBooks. Then I refined my selection to the health, fitness, and dieting category, and there were over 1500 books available. It helps to read the reviews and check over the book before you get started reading to ensure this

book provides the type of information you are looking for, but it is a good way to gain knowledge, check out a topic or determine if you want to read more from a particular author.

Check out free book promotion groups/sites.
Another way to find free books is to find Internet groups, like Facebook groups, that are specifically formed for promoting free eBooks. In these groups, each day there will be posts showing the books that are free and the dates the free books are available. The post will list the dates the book is offered free as well as a link to the download site. The quality of the books may vary, but it is often possible to find some great free books this way.

Read a library book/eBook.
Another way to get free books is to get a local library card and go to your library. If you don't have the time to make trips to the library or if you prefer eBooks, then you can follow the procedure to download eBooks from your local library.

Listen to podcasts.
Podcasts are another form of information. A podcast is a combination of the words iPod and broadcast. If you are not already familiar with podcasts, they are audio presentations on different topics. There are many podcasts available to download that will give you information or advice on just about any topic. There are also many podcasts that are inspirational. Many of them are free. To find podcasts, you can search online using the keyword "podcast" and your topic of interest, or check out the many podcast apps available.

Sign up for a Massive Open Online Course.
Did you know that there are sites online that offer online college courses taught by some of the top universities and professors in the country, and many of these courses are free? They are called MOOC's, or Massive Open Online Courses. Did you always want to learn about photography or graphic design? Do you want to learn how to write a novel or start a business? Do you want to learn how to write computer code? Do you want to learn about

cooking or fitness? Do you want to learn about public speaking, early childhood or finance? Now you can. Many of the courses consist of a number of short videos, and although they often have a time frame for watching them, you can usually watch at your own pace as long as you are only interested in the knowledge and not signed up to obtain a certificate. Some of the sites that offer the courses are Coursera.org and EdX.org, but there are many more.

Join an online group.
There are many online groups, including Facebook groups, that are full of people with the same interests as you, who are happy to share their knowledge and help out others who are interested in learning more about their topics of interest. I have found this to be a great way to connect with others of similar interests, differing backgrounds, and multiple experience levels to get my questions answered quickly. Often the members are from all over the world, so even if I'm working late into the night, someone is usually there to help me out. If I leave a question before I go to bed, I often wake up and find many solutions and links to help me with my question. It is important to always try to give back to the group by offering advice to members when you are able to, and always follow the group's rules that are posted on the group's page.

Find a mentor.
Mentors are another great resource for continued learning. A mentor is a person who is doing what you are doing or would like to do. It may be a teacher you had in the past, a connection on social media, a friend, an expert, or anyone you ask. Mentoring can take on many forms and time frames. It can extend from simple email correspondence or 15-minute phone calls once a month all the way up to a full internship. One of the best ways to decide if you are interested in pursuing a new interest or a new line of work is to talk to someone who currently does the job you are interested in, to find out the ins and outs and all the details. Then, it may be easier to decide if it

sounds like something you would like to pursue before you spend a great deal of time learning every detail. You can evaluate many aspects of a potential career to see if there are any surprises or decide if you want to even pursue that career or not, once you have more details. There is nothing like advice from someone who's been there. You may want to talk to several people because everyone and every experience is different; that way, you will get several different views. I gained so much knowledge from the mentors in my life. I learned about things you couldn't get out of a book or research paper. I learned from experiences, words, friendships and reflections just to name a few. Try it; you'll be glad you did!

Locate free trainings.
Other ways to expand your knowledge include watching free lectures, auditing a class, and watching free webinars. Free webinars can be easily found by searching online using the keywords free webinar and a topic of your choice, such as nutrition, meditation, marketing, social media, fitness etc. Remember to always try to select the ones that appear to be from reputable sources. Often, libraries and teaching institutions offer free lectures, so check their websites or give them a call. If they don't offer something on your topic of interest, you may spark the idea for them or they will direct you where to go to get the information you are seeking. Check with your local colleges about auditing classes. You may even want to contact a professor that teaches a topic you are interested in to see if you can sit in on a class.

Reach out to others.
Try contacting others for information you require. Many people love to share their expertise and help others. Talk to a counselor in the adult education office of your local college to find out what may be available besides paid college courses. Email or talk to professors at your local community college. I did that a few years ago.

One day, I was sitting on the back deck of our house and heard a buzzing sound. I looked up and could not believe what I saw. Every window on the upper level of the house was covered with some sort of winged insect the size of a bee. I looked at all the surrounding houses and there was nothing. My first thought was, "Am I in a horror movie?" and my second thought was, "What's up with our house?" Often, as evening rolled around, many of our neighbors would take walks around the neighborhood and I was sure they wouldn't be able to miss the massive swarm of insects. I ran up to the upstairs of the house and inspected the bugs from inside. They were layered on top of each other and totally covered every upstairs' window. I took a picture of one to send to my husband. We thought we had bees or something worse and decided to call an exterminator. I also went on a university website and emailed a professor who was an expert on this topic because I worried that the bugs could be the beautiful fireflies that we enjoyed looking at in the field behind our house and I didn't want to harm them. The university professor emailed me back to tell me that the photo I sent was a picture of a cicada. They are fascinating bugs that emerge in 17- and 13-year cycles and are mentioned in literature, art, songs and folklore. The professor shared that because this event is so amazing, he and his colleagues sit out and observe the show for the few weeks the insects emerge. I was so grateful to have the valuable information the professor provided. I could sense his passion when I read his detailed email. I cancelled the exterminator and felt honored to enjoy the last week of their show. I was so glad I reached out for information and did not exterminate the fascinating cicada.

Attend an information sharing meet-up.
There are meet-ups related to many topics available. If you cannot find one in your area, consider starting your own with a group of friends or colleagues with similar interests. If you are working, you could even start a meet-up over your lunch hour once a week or month if your employer allows it. If you are at home, you could meet with others after school drop-off or even

while having a play date. You may be surprised by how many people share your same interests.

Select the topics to learn about.
Now that you have identified the steps you plan to take to work toward your goals by filling out the *Mind Map Worksheet* and/or the *Action Plan Worksheet* from chapter five, it will be easier to determine the topics you would like to learn more about. There may be topics you need more knowledge in to move forward or topics you are just interested in learning more about. If you did not fill out the *Mind Map Worksheet* and/or *Action Plan Worksheet,* review chapter five and any other chapter you may need to reread in order to complete the worksheets. Once you have that information, fill out the *Learning Topics and Interests Worksheet* at the end of this chapter by listing the topic and the specific information about the topic you would like to acquire to help you get closer to achieving your goal.

Plan how and when you will proceed.
Once you have listed the topics you want to gain more knowledge about on the *Learning Topics and Interests Worksheet*, you will need to determine how and when you will obtain the information. Fill out the *My Daily Learning Worksheet* at the end of the chapter to help you organize your continual learning time. Try to include a small bit of learning each day if possible. Use the smart hacks discussed in this chapter, and don't forget to include continued learning when needed as you fill out your next day's *Daily Plan Worksheet,* which was included in chapter seven.

You can even get started by selecting one or two learning techniques that fit into your newly defined schedule to increase your knowledge today. You will be amazed at how much you can learn while still fitting it into your current schedule. Remember to be creative. If you can double up, for example, by exercising while listening to a podcast or watching a video while you're waiting at your child's music lesson, you may need very little or no additional time to learn what you need to move forward and grow. You will gain knowledge, feel inspired and feel more confident, so start now. Happy learning!

HOW LEARNING TO LOVE LEARNING HELPS YOUR CHILD

Learning can improve all aspects of your life. You will feel more knowledgeable and more confident, be able to converse on multiple topics, share information with others, and everything you learn will not only help you, but it will help your family. When you share your learning topics and details about interesting things you learned, you may interest others in your family and inspire them to learn more about that topic too. But most of all, one of the greatest benefits you can provide for your child is to model the importance of learning, as well as the excitement it can provide.

I don't know about you, but sometimes when I think back to my school days, I remember sitting in certain classes and impatiently waiting for the bell to ring. I would be thinking, "Why in the world do I need to know about this topic, and how does it affect me?" In other classes, I was more interested and enjoyed the class. One of the differences I observe as I look back at those experiences was the fun way the teachers approached the topics and made learning exciting by relating it to everyday life. I didn't really know that learning was a lifelong exciting process back then. I just wanted to graduate. I also did not know that although several topics I was taught about in school didn't excite me, there was an infinite number of topics in the world that I could learn about that would be of great interest to me. Now, think of the message that you can model and share with your children about the multitude of ways to learn and the super exciting things there are in the world to learn about. It is good to know that you don't have to like every topic that exists, but it's important to know that you do grow from each topic you learn about, and while you may not think you enjoy a particular topic, there is usually one aspect of just about any topic that would interest you if you were aware of it. When you begin to feel excitement about a particular topic, you are headed in the right direction.

Talk to your child about what excites them.
Talk to your child about the exciting things you are learning about, and ask them to share what excites them about learning. This will show your child that you are interested in them, and it will provide the opportunity to discover what excites your child. Watch their face and gestures as they discuss each topic. Ask questions, share your own stories and show your own excitement about learning. When they are excited, acknowledge it and explain how great it is that learning continues throughout life and how sad it would be if we couldn't learn new things. Getting excited about learning can help your child feel happier and more confident.

Link enjoyable topics to others.
Having these discussions with your child can also be a great way to find out their learning style and interests and help them with the topics they do not enjoy. You can do this by linking the topic they do not enjoy to one of their interests or a topic they do enjoy. If your child doesn't like history but is greatly interested in science and how mechanical things work, you may decide to help them find a book, video or just discuss with them how mechanical items evolved over time. Focus on the areas they are interested in but expand a bit to include how the period of time impacted the mechanical invention. This discussion may spark an interest in understanding more about different periods of history and what was happening at that time. An example would be, how the invention of electricity affected mechanical design or how the invention of the steam engine affected transportation and the lives of the people living at that time. There is always a creative angle to take to expand your child's interest in just about any topic. If your child has an assignment to create a project related to history, help them explore topics in history that are related to a subject they are greatly interested in. Younger children may need a bit of help making the connection

whereas older children may just need the suggestion to get the connection.

Uncover exciting facts.
Another way you may interest your child in a topic they may not enjoy is by explaining exciting facts about the topic they may not have considered at all. If your child comes home unhappy because they have to give a presentation on bugs and thinks their friend who was assigned a sports presentation has a much more exciting topic, help your child understand their topic can also be very exciting. Help your child find facts about their topic that are exciting or not well known. This can be as simple as doing an Internet search for interesting facts about the topic. During this search about insects, they may find out about the cicadas' cycles or a number of other fascinating facts that may kick-start their excitement with their project. Don't forget to help your child find reliable sources and appropriate sites whenever they research their topic.

Share age-appropriate smart hacks with your child.
Share some of the smart hacks from this chapter with your child. Make sure the hack is safe and appropriate for your child's age. Even though it may be ok for your high school age child to join a writing group online if they are aware of Internet safety rules, can be trusted to follow them, and have occasional supervision, it is not appropriate to let your seven-year-old search the Internet and join groups on their own. Some of the smart hacks can be used with guidance and supervision, such as contacting a college professor or finding an appropriate free book or podcast, or even finding an approved mentor. As your child gets a little older, ask your child to create a list of topics they are interested in learning more about or learning how to do. You may want to do the same and share your list with your child. This may help you find topics you enjoy together. As your child gets older, don't forget to share the ever-expanding list of old and new smart

hacks you pick up as they become age-appropriate. You may find your child may even have some to share with you!

Support continual learning.
Including continual learning as a family topic will show your child that leaning is ongoing and doesn't only happen in school. Discuss continual learning at the dinner table. Take turns having each family member share something new they learned, along with the source of the information. This will highlight the multitude of learning available and will even allow the younger children to join in.

One way you can show your child the benefits of continual learning would be to help your child locate and view an online training video about something they have an interest in learning about. Maybe they would like to learn how to play guitar, how to perform a cool science trick, or learn how something works. It is a great substitute for TV watching on a rainy day, and your child will benefit from increasing their knowledge and you will gain more insight into their interests.

Encourage your child's interests.
While it is important to encourage your child to expand their interests, it is also important to support the topics they currently enjoy. Help your child find activities and groups related to their interests. If your child is fascinated by building things, let them attend a Lego building session at the library, a robotics summer school class or take them to a parent-child resource center that has gigantic blocks to play with. You can also do this by collecting boxes of all sizes and letting them play with them or build massive towers in the yard with their friends. Other ways to do this is to ask a local builder if they would talk to your child about their job and the tools they use, take trips by a new house being built and watch the progress, have your child plan and build a similar structure with popsicle sticks, or watch a video with your child about building a dog house and then build one together. There are so many ways to inspire a child's interest

and share in the excitement. You may also create memories you will cherish forever.

Sharing a love of learning with your child can be one of the greatest gifts you can give them. This gift will travel with them throughout life and create continual growth and a thirst for more.

LEARN TO LOVE LEARNING REVIEW

1. You do not need to have prior knowledge about the topic you want to pursue to take action. You can learn along the way.
2. Technology is your friend, whether you're comfortable using it or not.
3. You don't have to make time for learning; you can fit it into your everyday schedule.
4. Learning can be as easy as entering a search word into your Internet browser.
5. Perma-free books are books that are always free to download.
6. Many authors periodically list their books for free in free book groups on social media sites like Facebook. The books are often listed with a convenient link directly to the download site.
7. You can borrow books and eBooks for free from most local libraries without leaving your home.
8. Podcasts are great to listen to while you are on the go or doing other things. You can find many podcasts for free.
9. MOOCs, also called Massive Open Online Courses, are often offered by top universities and professors, and many are free. Some sites that offer MOOCs are EdX.org and Coursera.org. They are usually split into small videos and allow you to watch at your own pace.
10. Online groups can be found in places such as Facebook and LinkedIn. The groups offer support, answer questions and provide information in specific areas of interest. Don't forget to follow the group rules before posting.
11. Mentors can take on many flexible arrangements and are a great resource.

12. Free webinars, auditing classes, contacting the adult education office in your area, emailing or talking to professors at your local community college, attending meet ups, conferences, and free lectures are all part of a list of growing ways to continually learn.

13. Reach out to others for advice or the information you require. Emails, phone calls, and connecting on social media are all ways to connect. Many people love to share their expertise and help others.

14. Evaluating the steps written on the *Action Plan Worksheet* and/or the *Mind Map Worksheet* that you filled out in chapter 5 will help you determine the additional knowledge you require to move forward.

15. Combining learning with other activities when safely possible can reduce the amount of additional time needed to move forward with your goals.

Learn to Love Learning Exercises

1. Think about your daily schedule and how you could fit in at least one piece of continual learning.

2. Review the smart hacks discussed in this chapter, and select one or two ways to start learning that will fit into your daily routine.

3. Fill out the *Learning Topics and Interests Worksheet* at the end of this chapter, after reviewing the *Mind Map Worksheet* and/or *Action Plan Worksheet* that you competed in chapter 5 and deciding which topics you need to learn more about to move forward with your goals. List the topics you will require more information about in order to move forward with your goals.

4. Plan for and include learning into your schedule on a weekly or daily basis, when possible, by using the *Daily Learning Worksheet* at the end of this chapter. Combine learning with other activities when safely possible. Start Learning!

5. Feel grateful that by continually learning, both you and your child will benefit.

Learn to Love Learning Exercises to Help Your Child

1. Model the importance of learning, as well as the excitement it can provide.
2. Talk to your child about the exciting things you are learning about and ask them to share what excites them about learning.
3. Explain to your child they don't have to like every topic that exists, but they will grow from each topic they learn about. When they have to learn about a topic in school that they are not interested in, find a way to link it to their interests, select a learning method they enjoy or research and explain fascinating facts about the topic they may not know.
4. When your child finds a topic uninteresting, try uncovering exciting facts about the topic your child did not know.
5. Ask your child to create a list of topics they are interested in learning more about or want to learn how to do. It may be fun to create and discuss your own list with your child. This may help you find topics you enjoy together.
6. Help your child research, locate and view an online training video about something they are interested in learning about. Examples include learning how to play guitar, how to perform a science experiment or how something works
7. Introduce the smart hacks discussed in this chapter and find out which methods of learning interest them most. This can be a great way to find about their learning styles and interests and later help them with the topics they do not enjoy.

8. Make a decision to include continual learning as a dinner topic each week. Have each family member share with the rest of the family something new they learned, along with the source of the information. This will highlight the many different sources of learning and will even allow the younger children to join in.

9. Encourage and support your child's interests by finding ways for them to explore their interests further through experiences, activities or groups that share the same interests.

10. Model and share a love of learning with your child. It can be one of the greatest gifts you give them. This gift will travel with them throughout life, creating continual growth and a thirst for more.

LEARNING TOPICS AND INTERESTS WORKSHEET

Continual learning will expand your mind, provide interesting topics of discussion and increase your knowledge. It will also help you reach your present goals and expedite any similar goals in the future. Look at the steps on your Action Plan and Mind Map worksheets and then document the topics you will need to learn more about in order to move forward with your goals.

Topic	Specific information needed
Example: Marketing my photography	How to advertise on Facebook

Now that you have documented the learning topics required to expand your knowledge and successfully propel you forward with your smaller goals, use this worksheet as you fill out your My Daily Learning Worksheet to plan when and how you will obtain the information.

YOU ARE ON YOUR WAY TO A BRIGHTER LIFE!

MY DAILY LEARNING WORKSHEET

Look at the topics listed on your *Learning Topics and Interests Worksheet* that will help you move forward with your goals. Think about what will propel you the fastest, as well as your time availability. Can you obtain this information while doing other things, or does it need your full concentration? Schedule daily learning topics.

Date	What I would like more information about today?	How I will obtain the information?	How will I schedule this into my day?	Done? Y/N
Jan. 1	Example: Advertising on Facebook	Listen to a 30-minute podcast on Facebook Marketing	I will listen to the podcast when I walk during my lunch break.	Yes

Now that you have decided on the information you would like to learn about, and have scheduled it into your day, nothing can stop you from becoming the infinite learning machine!

CHAPTER 10

GRAB YOUR BONUS TIPS AND TOOLS

Now it is time to share with you some of my favorite tips and tools! This is one of my favorite chapters. This chapter could easily be expanded into an entire book. You will be amazed at how many different ways there are to get support and move forward whether you are working toward a personal goal or a business goal. Although some of the tools in this chapter address moms who are or who want to be entrepreneurs, don't skip over them because as you will see, many of the tips and tools can also be applied to your personal life. It is all a part of continual learning. You will also discover that there are many ways to use a tool that appears to be business-related for personal goals. If you can't use some of the tools yourself, you may be able to help someone else by sharing the information with them. I love to share this list with others because there is always a golden nugget or two that creates excitement. I have been helped by all these tips and tools over and over again, and now I am excited to share them with you.

Hire a freelancer.
When I wrote my first children's book series, I had a specific idea in mind for my main character. Although my mother was a talented artist, I did not follow suit. I do not illustrate at all. I wanted to have input into the design, so I went online to a freelancer site, read the instructions and put in a project request. I had never done this before and did not know anything about the process. I had no idea what the going rate for illustrators was, so I left the bidding up to the illustrators. I was a bit

nervous about the process and what price the illustrators would be asking, but I did it anyway because I was eager to get my book finished. I worried that the price would be way out of my range and I would unintentionally insult those who replied, but I faced that fear and did it anyway. I received over 30 replies, and when I looked at their portfolios, I was surprised to find that the quality of their work was really good. The price range of the offers varied greatly but I selected the illustrator that I both liked the best and could afford, and I ended up getting wonderful illustrations for five of my books from this illustrator. The relationship worked out great. About a year later, I was contacted by the freelance website regarding the experience I had while using their site. I submitted the information about my personal experience of finding an illustrator for my book series. I was surprised that I was selected to be a case study for the site and ended up getting back half the money I paid out as a reward for being selected. I shared the money with the illustrator and could not have had a better experience. Imagine the different outcome I would have had if I let my fear and lack of experience stop me! The process to search for a freelancer was free, so what did I have to lose? Better yet, look what I had to gain!

Freelance websites are found online, and they are a great way to get work done. Freelancers will create marketing messages for you, format your written words for book publishing, and create videos, audios, illustrations, and company logos just to name a few of the services they provide. Some sites have people who will do research for you, find email addresses, or locate professional contacts in your area of work. Freelance sites are not just for business purposes; they can also help you find unique items such as fun personalized videos for a birthday gift, someone to update your resume or a list of 20 great ideas for a four-year-old's birthday party. I have used them for personal purposes many times. If you imagine it, you can usually find someone who will do it for you!

Some of the sites also offer contests. When setting up a contest, a specific request for a particular item is made and freelancers submit their work by the specified deadline you select. Once the date is reached, the person who set up the contest can then select the work they like best. I did this for a logo design once and had over 35 beautiful logos to choose from.

I could not even begin to mention every service that is possible to purchase from a freelancer. There are many! Price ranges can vary from about five dollars to any price you are willing and able to pay. I find this a very reasonable way to get work done quickly, and to also outsource work I do not have the skills or desire to do. Many freelance sites will hold the payment in escrow until all work has been satisfactorily delivered. For larger projects, payment can be released in increments.

Find a student in training.
Another great resource is your local college. Often, there are college students looking to gain experience, get their name on something professional and make a bit of extra money. For example, the Art Department may know a graphic design student who would like to earn money creating your logo or creating a drawing from a photo of your grandmother for a special birthday gift. The Marketing Department may know a student who is interested in helping you with social media or your advertising campaign. Contacting the college division for the area in which you are looking for help is another excellent source of services. It also benefits the student by providing real-life experience for their resume.

Check out SCORE.
One of the best resources for small businesses that I know of in the United States is SCORE.org. This organization provides free business advice, assistance with business plans and also free mentoring either by email, phone or in person, for small businesses and entrepreneurs. The wealth of information on the website is immense. SCORE mentors are professionals, many of whom have successfully worked for years in their profession. Often, you can find major company CEOs and many extremely successful professionals who want to help others with the

experience they have gained throughout their careers. This experience is often unbeatable and the information is free. You can look on the SCORE website and read the qualifications of the mentors before you select one to ensure the person you select has the experience you are looking for. Once I emailed a mentor just to run my idea of a business by him. He sent back a very detailed response that included many considerations I had never even thought about. The resources provided are extremely valuable. I am always impressed at the level of expertise I find. The site also offers many free webinars and even provides awards for new businesses that excel. If you don't do anything else in this chapter, check out the SCORE.org site if you are planning on researching an idea or starting any type of business.

Look for an accountability associate.
It is very important to be accountable when trying to reach a goal, whether it is to lose weight, start an online business or create your masterpiece. Accountability includes making a measurable commitment to a group or individual in order to stay on task and accomplish desired goals and then keeping that commitment.

Having a friend, partner, mentor, or group who believes in you and your goals is often the key to success. There are many ways to be accountable such as sending out a weekly email with the tasks you plan to complete that week, making an accountability phone call, talking face to face, or any other way you can let an accountability associate or group know that you made a commitment and intend to take specific actions to keep that commitment.

The most important part of the accountability process is to make a commitment, share it, then follow up to explain if it was completed, and if it was not, why it was not completed. Remember to be 100 percent accountable and don't use excuses. Sometimes as you work on your goals, you may hit an obstacle, find out that there is a better direction to go in, or experience an emergency that prevents you from keeping your commitment, but being accountable is important. Reporting to others whether your commitment was kept and if not, why not, will keep you on track with your goals and increase your success rate.

Join or start a mastermind group.
Mastermind groups are another great source of information and support. They are usually small groups that help the members overcome obstacles through the collective intelligence of others who share similar goals. The mastermind process includes members seeking advice or feedback for a particular issue, brainstorming ways to help each member with their challenge and expressing gratitude to the other members for their help and support. I belong to a mastermind group that has provided me with tremendous support and invaluable information. You can find groups by searching the Internet or starting your own mastermind group.

These groups meet regularly by conference call, virtually or in person, and the participants follow a set routine to discuss their goals. The process, includes sharing successes since the last meeting, as well as what each group member is currently working on, then requesting advice, which often leads to a brain storming session. At the end of the meeting each member makes a commitment to stretch a little out of his or her comfort zone by completing a task related to the member's goal by an agreed upon date. This process is a very successful way to move forward, receive support, maintain accountability and gather ideas from others who may provide different ideas or views than you do. The members provide honest, gentle feedback, and each member is safe to share their thoughts and dreams without any fear of judgment whatsoever. There have been times in the past when I have been really stuck on one idea and after bringing it to my group, I found a great solution that I hadn't ever considered. Often, members of the group have diverse experience and can really help each other succeed. This mastermind process is helpful for members with many diverse goals including losing weight, training for a marathon, looking for employment or starting a business.

A mastermind group is also beneficial when facing obstacles and fear. In the mastermind group that I belong to, when a fear-inducing commitment is made to the group, we provide support between the calls through Facebook posts or quick emails to assist the member who is facing the fear. This is helpful and also increases accountability. It's nice to know that others can really relate to what you are experiencing and are rooting for your success!

Conduct research and interviews others.
Another way to get feedback regarding a project you may be working on or considering working on is to interview others who are experiencing the same situation or are in the same target group or niche you are focusing on. Often, we think we know what is important for others, but what we are usually doing is confusing what we think should be important for others with what is important to us. Before writing this book, I interviewed many parents to find out their ideas, opinions and needs. I asked many questions including the challenges of being a parent and the magic solutions parents would wish for if their wish would be granted. I am a parent, and although I have had many experiences over the years, I know everyone's experiences differ and the more information I collect, the more I ensure that parents relate to my book.

An example of how researching and interviewing could be used with personal decisions would be if you were deciding whether to hire a babysitter or to use a daycare. In this example, it would benefit you to look at your unique situation first, and then research the benefits and drawbacks of both options. You could also ask others who are in similar situations or have used both, about their experiences and what they like and dislike about each option. Then, you can base your decision on your individual situation and the information you have obtained.

It is important to ask the questions and also look for the patterns to find the information to help you succeed. I never fail to find out something in each interview that I had never previously considered, and it opens my eyes just a bit wider.

Create an online survey or poll.
Another great resource is online surveys or polling. There are free and paid websites that offer simple tools to create surveys. Many of the social media sites also have polling options. I recently used the survey resource when selecting the title of my Maxi Mom Success Mentoring System. I listed several titles that I came up with, along with an option for the polltaker to write in a title suggestion, then asked people to select the title they liked best. This can also be used for personal requests on social media for selecting a date for a baby shower or finding out what food people prefer for a dinner party or even considering a new haircut! Polling is quick and easy and a good way to get a question answered. Just remember to make sure you are polling the people who are in your target area if that applies. It may not help to target a knitting site about a poll related to skateboarding.

Hire a virtual assistant.
If things get very busy, you need help and your budget allows it, you can even hire a virtual assistant, also known as a VA. There are sites online where you can hire a VA for an hour, several hours per day, full-time or for one small task. It is even possible to completely automate a business by paying others to do the tasks required for the entire job. Many virtual assistants can be found on the freelancer sites and by searching the keyword "virtual assistant." It may even be possible to hire a VA to perform the main tasks in your business. If you hire professional virtual workers you can rely on, with the correct knowledge, you may be able to hire one or more VAs to successfully run a large portion of your business.

If you decided to run a logo business, you would not necessarily have to know how to actually create the logos yourself if you have one or more virtual assistants that could. Once a client orders a logo from you, the virtual assistant could take it from there. When the logo is complete and payment is received, you could keep a percentage of the money and pay your designer the rest. If you use your imagination, you can do as little or as much as you have the time or desire to do. What other ideas could you come up with that could follow a similar path?

Ask.
Another great tip that I'd like to share with you, consists of just one simple word, but can bring you so much success you will not believe it. The simple word is ASK. Don't be afraid to ask for items, assistance or advice! Ask for what you need and don't let fear stop you. This one tip will get you further than any other tip. It will help you in every area of your life. Don't fear the word, just watch for the surprises you will receive when you just ask.

Asking is one thing that I never did until I learned this tip. I used to consider myself shy while growing up, and the thought of asking for anything scared me tremendously. Since learning this great tip, I have asked for and received upgrades to oceanfront hotel rooms, shorter workweeks, discounts, free advice, professional connections, interviews and more. I would estimate that more than three quarters of the time when I have asked for things, I have received what I asked for or better, and my greatest fear of all—feeling embarrassed—has never happened.

My experience has been that when a request is presented in a polite inquiring way, even if it is turned down, it has been turned down in a very gentle and professional way. Often, the reason for denying the request related more to the person's inability to make that type of decision in the position they held, or because the item or service I requested was not available. I have also found that even when I have been turned down, I was still presented with other options or told to check back at a later time.

One time I asked for an upgrade on a family vacation and was told on the phone there were none available. When we arrived, I was told that because I had inquired and had stayed there before, and because they just had a cancellation, I could have a larger oceanfront suite with access to the member's lounge on that floor where food and drinks were served every evening for free! Another time, I asked a store manager for money off the price of a picture I wanted to buy because it had a small crack in the frame, and I ended up getting the picture and frame for free. Don't forget the story I told you earlier in the book, about how I asked and was allowed to work fewer days for the same pay. Believe me it doesn't hurt to ask!

It also can be beneficial to do a bit of research if you are making an important request. For example, if you were looking for a writing mentor, and really wanted to ask a known author, or maybe even your favorite author, it helps to be prepared. You may benefit by doing a little research, practicing your request, being clear about the expectations of the request and limiting the time commitment of the person you are planning to ask, and who knows you may just end up with the mentor of your dreams.

Find a coach or mentor.
Let's talk a bit more about mentors and coaches. Coaching or mentorship is another way to receive support, knowledge, feedback and advice. Coaching or mentoring can take place as often or as infrequent as needed. It can be solely individual coaching or individual coaching combined with group meetings, trainings and other helpful methods. You can have a coach whom you call to prepare for a specific one-time task or someone you talk to daily or monthly, as well as many variations in between. Mentors and coaches work in many areas, including fitness, nutrition, leadership, parenting, meditation and more. Although I have had many great coaches, Jack Canfield's Train the Trainer and Success Coaching propelled me on my way to where I am today and provided the experience that I needed to write this book and continue to help others.

If there is something you would like to do, I can guarantee there is someone else out there who has already done it, has done something similar, or has expertise in parts of the process. A mentor or coach can provide advice based on years of successful experience and they can greatly accelerate your progress to the outcome you desire. You don't have to spend years of trial and error and repeat the same mistakes if someone else already did it and can provide you with a much shorter path. Finding the process that works the best for your style and your schedule will greatly benefit you.

When making a mentoring request, be clear on the specific details of the request and respect the other person's time. Although I recommend having some type of prior relationship with the person you will be asking to mentor you, it is not essential. One way to approach a request is to briefly explain your project and what you admire about this person, state why you selected them, and make your clear request. An example of a clear request to a marketing mentor might be to ask the mentor if they would agree to answer five questions by way of a once a month email exchange, a twice a month ten-minute call, etc. The clearer you are, the better the chance you will get the answer you want to receive. If the person you are asking is not clear about your request or interprets it to mean you are asking for more of their time than they can provide, the potential mentor may turn you down without asking for further clarification. If you are turned down, politely thank them, don't take it personally and ask someone else. There are many experts out in the world.

Learn how obstacles can be helpful.
Another helpful tip I want to share is that obstacles and rejections are helpful! Yes you heard me right. If you are moving right along and not encountering obstacles, or any rejection at all, then you are not stretching yourself and you may not even be moving at all!

Obstacles and rejections are growth and learning experiences. Think back through your life. I bet you can come up with some great things that happened to you after you changed direction or hit a roadblock and had to figure out what to do next. You may not have realized it at the time, but you may see it now when you look back over the experience. You have made it through every day of your life so far, and I know you have met challenges throughout your life. We all have. Accept the challenge, know that you have risen to the challenge, persevered many times already, and don't let it stop you as you move forward.

Plan a day of fun!
The last tip I want to include for you is a very important one. You're almost finished with the book. You've filled out the worksheets, practiced the tips and learned about many tools and resources. Now it's time to celebrate you and your family and plan a day of fun! Congratulations if you've started to take action and are working hard toward your goals, After all, wasn't working toward your goals one of the many important messages in this book? Well yes, but a happy, grateful, well-rounded life includes time to relax, enjoy family and other relationships, and have fun. So, using the *Day of Fun Worksheet* at the end of the chapter, plan a day to relax, enjoy life and celebrate the moment. Continue this practice on a regular basis. Put everything else out of your mind. Enjoy the moment and live! This will not only help you decrease stress but it will re-energize you too. Get excited, plan some playtime and just have fun. You deserve it!

You are now aware of many tips and tools that will help you face challenges better than you ever have before. *The Bonus Brainstorm List Worksheet* at the end of the chapter can also help you when you feel stuck. It includes many of the tips covered in this book as well as a few extra. Don't forget to research any of the resources you would like more information about, since my intent for this chapter was to provide a brief introduction to resources you may not have been aware of. Use the additional space on the worksheet to write in other tips you are aware of as well as the tips you discover in the future.

As you move forward and take action toward your goals and the life of your dreams, you may have to learn something new, or you may require help from others. Maybe a freelancer, an accountability associate, a mastermind group, a mentor or a coach will help you. Maybe you will interview others who are experts or have experienced the same situation. And don't forget to ask! People love to help others and share their knowledge, so if you feel stuck, brainstorm and use your newly acquired knowledge, and soon you may find there is something better waiting at the next turn or up the next few steps to the top. For every person who tells you no, there are many other people out there who will say yes. You just have to keep asking until you find them. Don't give up; you may be only one ask away from yes. It may take 101 asks to achieve your dream, but if you stop at 100, you will never get there, will you?

HOW GRABBING YOUR BONUS TIPS AND TOOLS HELPS YOUR CHILD

Many of the tips and tools can help you free up additional time and create more quality time to spend with your family. For example, if you successfully use some of the tips and tools, such as accountability associates, freelancers, asking and mentoring to help you reach your goals sooner or decrease the time you spend working on them, the time-savings can provide additional time for you to spend with your family.

Some of the tips and tools can also benefit your child directly. There are many ways the tips in this chapter can be incorporated into your home life. You can share the tips and tools that you are using with an older child to provide real life examples of how they can be used. This is especially helpful when there are tips or tools your child may not be aware of. You can even introduce some of the tips to a young child in very simple ways, as you will see below.

Teach your child to be accountable.
Learning about accountability is important at any age. This simple concept can be explained at a very young age. It can be as simple as telling a young child that they can get one popsicle out of the freezer and then asking the child to come back to mom or dad with the popsicle after they get it, to show they did exactly what they said they would do. Praise your child for doing exactly what they said they would do and tell them that when someone does what they say they will do, they are being accountable.

For an older child, accountability could include committing to and completing a major school project or a major room cleaning within the planned time period, after telling you the promised date that the project would be completed. It could also be coming home from a friend's house at the time you requested. This is an important process for children to learn and will help them throughout life.

Introduce the mastermind process to your child.
The mastermind process is a healthy decision-making process that can be shared with your child. It can be used when solving problems, planning goals or even when deciding what to do during summer vacation. It can take place around the dinner table while you eat or at a more official family meeting. It can include children of all ages. You would be surprised by the ideas a young child may come up with while brainstorming. This can also help a younger child feel like they can be an integral part of the group just as much as the older children. The techniques used in a mastermind group provide blueprints for your child's successful decision making and planning throughout life.

Teach your child about interviews and surveys.
Interviews and surveys are great tools for older children to learn about and can help them see that not everyone thinks or experiences things the same. Interviews and surveys also can help them notice trends and make logical assumptions which can be really helpful while working on school projects or at many other times in their lives. Even little children can learn this concept. When the family votes on topics, such as what movie to watch or where to go for a treat, make sure you are open to all the possible choices or provide select choices when using this voting process with young children.

Explain why asking is an important skill.
Let your child know that the word *ask* is an important word that everyone should know about. Tell them that throughout life, there will be times when they may have to ask others to help them and that is ok. You may even want to provide examples of when you have had to ask someone for help as well as times when you just

asked for something you wanted. Don't forget to share the outcomes as well. Tell them there is no harm in asking, and they should not feel guilty for asking for help when they truly need it or when they really want something. It is really a great tool for children to learn, especially when they have really thought about the rationale behind their request. If they can master this skill early, as well as understand that the answer won't always be yes, and that's ok; they will have one less fear to overcome and will experience a much richer life because of it.

Explain how obstacles can be helpful.
Share with your child the message that obstacles can be beneficial. When your older child faces an obstacle, you can tell them that although most people don't like obstacles, if people never experienced them, they wouldn't grow and learn from them or find other methods of getting the results we would like to see. Explain that everyone experiences obstacles in their life and even though they may not think about it, they have already been successfully finding ways around obstacles for years. Then point out a few obstacles that your child was challenged by and successfully overcame. You can even go further and have a discussion about other people who have overcome obstacles such as famous athletes or physically challenged classmates and how it helped them grow.

Teach your child the importance of fun.
The last tip is to remind your child that it is great to work hard and realize their goals and dreams, but it is also important to celebrate life. Model ways to celebrate and enjoy life and family. Let your child help you fill out the *Day of Fun Worksheet* or give them their own copy to fill out to plan their own day of fun on a mutually selected date in the future. Help your child celebrate accomplishments and discuss how they would like to contribute to family fun time.

Each time you add a new tip or tool to your *Bonus Brainstorm List Worksheet*, don't forget to share it with your child in whatever age-appropriate way you can. This list is ever-changing and always growing, so keep it handy, in your purse or as an electronic list on your phone or computer and keep adding to it and sharing it with your child. Even though my children are older, we still discuss the cool tips, apps and tools we discover. Anything that can save you or your child a few extra minutes and allow either of you to have less stress or more time to spend doing something you love is worth sharing.

GRAB YOUR BONUS TIPS AND TOOLS REVIEW

1. There are an infinite number of tips, tools and support available for you to use as you work toward your goals.
2. Freelance websites can be found online. They are great resources for getting work done, finding unique gifts or discovering creative ideas.
3. College students are often looking for real-life experience and extra money.
4. SCORE is an organization supported by the U.S. Small Business Administration and offers free, highly experienced mentors in a variety of fields, as well as webinars, information and advice in many areas. Their website is www.score.org
5. Accountability includes making a measurable commitment to a group or individual in order to stay on task and accomplish desired goals.
6. A mastermind group is a group of people who meet regularly, usually by phone, virtually or in person and follow a set routine, which includes, support, advice, brainstorming and accountability.
7. Interviews can provide information about a target group's hopes, opinions and problems, as well as a way to identify trends and commonalities.
8. Surveys are a good way to poll your target group and make decisions based on feedback.
9. Virtual Assistants can help with tasks that you have no time to do or no interest in doing.
10. Asking is one of the greatest skills to develop, often providing wonderful results.

11. Hiring a coach or finding a mentor can help you rise to the next level much quicker. Coaching or mentoring can be done individually, in a group or as a combination of the two.

12. Trainings such as webinars, conferences and podcasts can help take you to the next level and provide you with new and helpful information.

13. Obstacles and rejection can actually be a good thing because they indicate you are moving in a forward direction and stretching to make progress.

14. It is important to live a balanced life. When you are working toward your goals, taking time out to celebrate life and having fun can increase happiness, decrease stress and energize you.

Grab Your Bonus Tips and Tools Exercises

1. Explore freelance websites.

2. Visit the www.Score.org website and read about all of the free available resources. Search the mentor area and read the bios of some of the mentors that may be helpful to you if you are thinking about starting a business or making decisions about your career.

3. Select a friend or coach to be your accountability associate for any personal or business goals or join a mastermind group.

4. Practice asking. If you have already started making small requests, build up to larger ones.

5. Email the author of this book about one tip or tool you learned about, one benefit your child experienced from the tips in this book, or one step you are proud of taking by using the contact form at www.beAmastermom.com. I will read every comment!

6. Review this chapter often as you progress through your journey, to remind yourself about all of the resources available to you as you continue to grow.

7. Use the *Bonus Brainstorm List Worksheet* at the end of this chapter to help you whenever you meet an obstacle or need a bit of help deciding what to do next.

8. Use the *Day of Fun Worksheet* at the end of the chapter to plan a special day of fun for you and your family! Celebrate life. You deserve it.

9. Feel grateful that by knowing helpful tips and receiving help and support from others, both you and your child will benefit.

Grab Your Bonus Tips and Tools Exercises to Help Your Child

1. Prepare to enjoy the additional time you save after using some of the bonus and time saving tips in this book.

2. Teach your child about accountability in an age-appropriate manner.

3. Introduce the mastermind process to your child, as a healthy decision-making process. Use it when solving problems, planning goals or even when deciding on where to take a day trip. It can take place around the dinner table while you eat or as a more official family meeting.

4. Teach the concept of voting and polling to a small child by using hand votes and to an older child by introducing interviews and surveys. This will help your child understand that not everyone thinks or experiences things the same.

5. Encourage your child to ask for what they want, especially when they need help with something. Explain that asking is a useful skill that often provides wonderful results.

6. Share with your child the message that obstacles can be beneficial and that everyone experiences obstacles. Point out a few obstacles your child successfully overcame. Include a discussion about other people who have overcome obstacles such as famous athletes or physically challenged classmates.

7. Model to your child ways to celebrate and enjoy life and family. Let your child help you fill out your *Day of Fun Worksheet* or give them their own copy to fill out to plan their own day of fun for a mutually selected date in the future.

DAY OF FUN

While you are working hard, don't forget to take a day to rest, reenergize or celebrate an achievement. Isn't loving life what it's all about?

You can schedule fun days on a routine basis or plan a special day for when you achieve one of your smaller goals as you make progress toward the big one! You can make it a "me" day or include family or friends.

Don't forget to use the Swap, Share or Ask method if you need to when planning some time for yourself!

It's time to grab a cup of coffee or tea, put your feet up and plan away!

Date of celebration event

Give a name to your day of fun!

What will you do? Get excited as you plan. Visualize and write down all the fun details of your special day! If it is a family day, you may want to include your children in the planning so they can get excited too!

Who will join in on the fun?

BONUS BRAINSTORM LIST WORKSHEET

Not sure where to turn or what to do next? It happens to all of us, including the most successful people ever. Sometimes, a short break will help clear the way. You can also use this handy brainstorm list of solutions to get you through the clouds. Remember, the most beautiful blue sky is right on the other side, so don't give in!

Hire a freelancer	Google and compare
High school/college student	Take a free online course
Score.org	Join a mastermind
Friend	Accountability partner
Partner	Create a Mind Map
Mentor	Complete daily reviews
Research the web	Prioritize
Conduct an interview	Coursera, EdX
Join a Facebook group	Title generator
Hire a coach	5 small steps a day
ASK	Targeted Facebook ad
Email a college professor	Social media scheduler

Create an online campaign	
Listen to a podcast	
Amazon free books	
Create an online poll	
Plan your daily tasks	
Join a group like MeetUp	
Swap with someone	
Delegate	
Share cost/task with others	
Visualize	
Start a group	
Provide free info to others	
Hire a young neighbor	
Take walk/clear your mind	

I'm certain that by now, you have come up with solutions that have worked for you that are not on the list, so don't forget to write in a few of your own great ideas!

CHAPTER 11

CELEBRATE THE NEW YOU

Wow, you made it to the last chapter of the book, and now you know the simple process to lead you toward the life you desire. This process can help you at any point in your life. If used successfully, it will help you if your goal is to lose weight, open a business, clean your garage, exercise more, or save money for a new outfit. The possibilities are endless.

As you start on your way toward any goal, don't worry if you end up starting in one direction and then decide to change directions, because as you learn more and more about yourself and the amazing endless opportunities that are out there, you may decide to embrace them too! This is the excitement of life and now you know it. You can achieve your goals. You can create the life of your dreams. It is all up to you and no one else. Setbacks can't stop you. Naysayers can't stop you. Negative self-talk won't stop you now. You don't need a Harvard degree to achieve. You don't need tons of money. You don't need a team of experts. Nothing can stop you from taking one small step after another to get to your proudest moment yet.

The greatest thing of all is that your child does not have to wait until adulthood to learn these wonderful secrets! Think about how great it would have been if you had learned all of the steps in this book at a very early age and had been using them for years. Imagine if each tip was now a well-formed habit you relied on every day without giving it another thought! This is what you will do for your child. That is the greatest gift of all. Welcome to the new you and to your exciting new life. Be proud, be happy, and be excited because you are on your way to something spectacular!

FEEL GREAT ABOUT YOUR PROGRESS

This is it, this is the time to look back at your progress so far. Don't be judgmental. Remember to squash that negative self-talk by replacing it with statement such as, "I am so happy that I am on my way to achieving my hopes and dreams!" and "I am so grateful that I can help lead my child to success."

You must follow your own path to success. Some people decide to complete the steps in the book as they read through it the first time, and others like to read the entire book to get the big picture, and then return to the beginning to start implementing the steps. Use this book as your guide and return to it over and over. Take notes, complete the worksheets, and mark your favorite pages. There is no right or wrong way to begin, because just by reading this book, you already took action! You already moved forward because you already gained knowledge. With that knowledge comes the confidence of knowing how to master any task, one small step at a time. You may decide that you want to read the book again, review the chapter exercises, share this information with a friend or even invite others to join you as you move forward. If you are interested in using this book to start a meeting or group to guide others, please request more information by completing the contact form at the website http://beAmastermom.com.

As you follow the steps in this book you may not notice at first, but others will begin to see the new you. They will see your increased confidence, extra passion for life, and your positive outlook. They may notice that things are going well for you and your family is thriving too, all because you took the first step by reading this book.

Keep the book handy. Refer to it often. Stay inspired. Travel at the pace that feels comfortable for you in your life but keep moving forward. Don't forget to be grateful, look for the positive, and take small continual steps, or even a big sprint when you feel like it. Don't forget to review the book often for the tips you were not ready to use at the beginning but can now benefit from after becoming more knowledgeable and progressing further toward your goal. Refer often to the *New You Checklist Worksheet* at the end of the chapter as a quick review of the tasks in this book and feel proud as you check off the tips you have already mastered.

If you ever find you are losing that passionate feeling, return to the earlier chapters and exercises. As you learn more and experience more, you will need to continually re-evaluate. That is a part of growing. Every bit of new information can point you in another direction that will lead you to the outcomes you desire.

That is exactly what happened to me. My energy and desires changed as I started toward one of my goals. I used to love to write children's books for fun. I never intended to publish them because it was just a fun activity that made me happy. Several years ago, I decided to become more serious about writing, so I combined my knowledge of early brain development research, developmental milestones and writing. I decided to write a children's book to help new parents learn important information about early development. Instead of just writing children's stories as I had in the past, I decided to also include a letter for parents in the front of the book. In the back of the book I included a list of newborn-related developmental milestones and activities to promote development.

As I proceeded with my goal and realized it was achievable, I decided I wanted to write several books, so parents would get information about age-related development starting right at birth and continuing to age three. That decision developed into a book series. I named the main character *Smart Art* and *The Art of Early Learning Series* was created. It was my passion that led me to the series. I never intended to create a series at first but as I moved forward, I expanded my goal.

While interacting with parents who enjoyed the book series, I found that while most parents not only wanted what was best for their children, they were also looking for ways to be happy themselves. I learned that parents want to follow their passion and spend more time with their children, without feeling overwhelmed with all the tasks they have to handle in their daily life. Although it took me years of career and personal experience to learn many of the tips in this book, I did not want other parents to have to wait that long to learn the helpful tips. Since my passion is helping others find happiness, writing this book was the next logical step for me. I became more excited when I realized that parents could help their children develop lifelong success habits in record time while progressing toward their own goals and desires. Then when I considered the benefits to the children from learning these powerful yet simple success tips so early in life, I could not control my excitement.

Once I started to hear the interest in this book and the number of people who were asking to read it before I was even half-finished, I realized I needed to do even more. My years of experience working with parents and children taught me that some people enjoy more guidance while learning and others are more independent learners. I always thought I was an independent learner, until I began taking part in success coaching and mastermind groups. This led me to the realization that I love to work alone at my own pace, and I love the freedom of being creative and planning my own strategies, but I also really love the feedback, guidance, fresh perspective, motivation and accountability that coaching and mastermind groups provide.

That insight is what led me to creating an online training, mentoring, professional accountability service and mastermind group that expands upon and reinforces some of the information in this book and provides one on one interaction. Realizing that different people require different options, led me to diversify my options so that every parent, regardless of desire, income, time and learning styles could get the support needed to move continuously forward at their own pace to achieve happiness and the life of their dreams. This all led to the development of the website www.beAmastermom.com.

It did not all happen at once! I had to learn things, get help from others, interview others and experiment as I traveled along this path. It was not hard, and anyone can do the same thing or anything else they desire by taking one small step at a time. Each step will help you feel accomplished and prove you can achieve while propelling you forward. Don't get me wrong, there will be obstacles, just like the ones I encountered, but remember, you learn from obstacles. As you maneuver around them you will feel proud and energized to move forward. Your new positivity will let you find the good that comes out of facing obstacles and moving forward.

So give yourself a pat on the back or a smile in the mirror and take a moment to celebrate yourself for taking the first step by reading this book. Celebrate each step that you take. Find others, i.e., groups, coaches, neighbors and friends, who are taking similar steps and share your achievements, big and small, because they will relate to you, encourage you and celebrate you! You will become the inspiration for others as they see your happiness, enthusiasm and passion for life. Your family, your child and best of all YOU will see and feel the difference each little step creates in your life, and you will know that you are providing your child with positive habits that can create a lifetime of success!

GET STARTED NOW

Here is my direct message to you to help you get started. You are unique and special in every way. I believe you can accomplish anything you want to accomplish. You know how to slice and dice your goals into small achievable pieces that you can easily fit into your routine. You're mastering life, and the knowledge you now possess will help you forever. The more you use the information in this book, the more natural it will become. You will become more confident and excited. You will know what you have accomplished and whether it is a small win or a large win, you should feel proud. You will develop great habits and you will succeed.

You will be more positive. Positivity will improve your day and make you much happier. You can decide your future and plan the exciting things you want to achieve. It doesn't matter if it's more time with your family, a new skill, your own business, passive income, a new hobby, a new relationship, a promotion, education, a new car or time for yourself. You possess the skills to make it happen, one step at a time.

Don't forget about the many free and low-cost resources out there to help you along the way. There are also mentors and supporters who will propel you along on your exciting journey; you don't have to do it alone. Share your excitement and accomplishments and inspire others along the way.

There will be times when life intervenes, when you fall out of the positive life you created, or you hit an obstacle and feel like giving up, and that's ok. It is expected to happen. It happens to me. It happens to everyone. Just realize that, take a short break and quickly get back on track in whatever way you can. Read the book again, do one small task you know will be a success in order to rebuild your self-esteem, brag a bit, make a list of your goals, visualize success, smile in the mirror for three minutes, or think about what you are grateful for, no matter how small you may feel it is at the time.

Read the daily affirmations listed on the *Inspiring Affirmations for Maxi Mom Success Worksheet* at the end of this chapter. You can also revise them or make up your own affirmations that are directly related to your goals. Affirmations are a way to state the goals that you would like to achieve as if you already achieved them. It is also a great way to keep your goals in the forefront of your mind. Carry them with you in your pocket or on your phone. Create an audio version to listen to as you drive to work or carry out daily tasks. Practicing affirmations at least daily, expressed in the present tense, can inspire and motivate you. Take a moment to feel the emotions you experience as you state each affirmation and believe in yourself. Some people read or state their affirmations when they get up each day and before they retire each evening as a powerful way to start and end each day.

Remember, it is all up to you. You can create the path that you travel. You can determine the life, the happiness and the success that you achieve. Don't forget that you are in control of how you feel, what you do, how you think and how you view the things that happen each day. Remember the story near the beginning of the book about the mom who put her baby to sleep at the end of the hectic day? Well don't forget, you can change the way you view things in just one second, just like the mom in the example.

Well I really want to thank you for allowing me to guide you through this book. As I have already shared, with you, my passion is helping others succeed. I came to this realization by using the same system described in this book. I then took little steps to break down my goals and over time I reached the goal that makes me very happy. That goal was to help others. I get to help others, see their success, help a future generation, and one by one make this world a slightly happier place. An added bonus is that I am following my passion. I feel confident. I am proud of my work. I enjoy every day and when I get off track, I notice it much quicker than I used to and then I quickly get myself right back on track.

I have also used this process to accomplish smaller goals such as helping homeless children, getting a new car and helping teen moms. I use it to plan trips, get upgrades, and in my everyday life. That is the beauty of it. These techniques can work for all goals, no matter how big or small. So go forward, reread the book, take notes, use the worksheets, share with others, highlight the meaningful text, but most importantly TAKE ACTION. Start small. Working toward your goals for just fifteen minutes a day can benefit you and help you get started toward the life you deserve. Come back as often as you need to and start this moment living the life of your dreams while preparing your child for a great future too! Enjoy the journey; it will be a great one!

HOW CELEBRATING THE NEW YOU HELPS YOUR CHILD

Your child will benefit by learning the skills you will be modeling, at an early age. What a great gift to give to your child. Your child will be aware of different methods that create results and successful ways to live a happier life even before entering school, if started early. Your child will know how to face obstacles and will know the benefits of asking for help from others. Your child will have tips that can help improve schoolwork and build confidence. If used often enough, the skills will turn into habits that can be relied upon for a lifetime.

Your child will also begin to experience a much happier you. Your child will learn from listening to you, watching you, copying your actions and even copying your attitude. The importance of modeling positive behavior to children has been documented time and time again. You may have experienced your child mirroring some of your slip-ups in the past, so it's now time to model the new you.

Research has shown that young children completing a task after watching their parents completing the same task often used the exact same actions as their parents even if those actions weren't necessary. In the research the parents were instructed to make many unnecessary actions before completing the task in front of their children. Even when the children were able to practice and successfully accomplished the task before their parents took part, once they observed the parent complete the unnecessary motions, they did the same. Children model their parents. This is well researched. As you become more confident, happy, positive and successful, and you can calmly face obstacles and perceived fear, you will be modeling many positive actions for your child.

Which is the better message to give to your child? "I'm so stressed I need a glass of wine" or "I'm a bit stressed, so I'm going to relax and listen to music for a few minutes because that helps me feel better." This is an example of how modeling positive words, actions and behaviors to your child, are so very important. Your positivity will help your child see the good in life. Your confidence will help your child feel safe, and assured that mom knows what's she's doing. Your child will observe you as you model how to take action, accept responsibility and not make excuses. Your child will see that you have dreams and goals, and will notice the steps you take to make them happen. Your child will see the pride when you reach a goal, the determination when you hit an obstacle, and the way you brainstorm other alternatives instead of giving up. Your child will see that learning can be fun and is a continual life process.

Your child will observe the many ways to learn, including using computers, reading books, talking with others, instructional videos and mentoring from others. Meals will turn into wonderful opportunities for you and your children to share your goals and dreams and help each other achieve them. Successfully modeling the tips in this book and successfully following the steps to introduce the same concepts in age related doses to your child would help develop habits that can benefit your child for a lifetime! Decide right now, to take your child by the hand and begin to walk together down the path toward the life you desire!

CELEBRATE THE NEW YOU REVIEW

1. You made it to the end of the book and you are on your way to something spectacular!
2. You now possess the knowledge to create just about anything that you want in your life.
3. As you learn and have new experiences you will want to readjust from time to time as your new knowledge, passion and skills help define the direction of your dreams. That is ok and that is expected.
4. Use this book as your guide and return to it over and over. Take notes, complete the worksheets, and mark your favorite pages. There is no right or wrong way to begin, because just by reading this book, you already took action!
5. There will be steps that you remember and use immediately and others that you may not need until later in the process so it is important to review the book and worksheets often.
6. The suggestions for how you can introduce the concepts to your child will vary depending on the age of your child, so return to the book to refresh your memory, as your child grows older.
7. Affirmations are a way to state the goals that you would like to achieve, as if you already achieved them. Affirmations can help inspire and motivate you.
8. Celebrate your progress big or small and don't let obstacles get in your way. Remember that obstacles make you better by teaching you things that will help and strengthen you and if you become part of a mastermind group or help a friend, you will be able to assist others when they encounter the same problem.

9. Keep moving forward one step at a time and enjoy the flow and the direction your path takes you.
10. Observe and enjoy the increased happiness, patience, confidence, sense of accomplishment, pride and love that you and your child feel as together you experience the life you were meant to live, all because you decided to take action and go for it!

Celebrate the New You Exercises

1. Smile then take one minute to feel proud of yourself for deciding to take action.
2. Set this book down and take that first small step to get started, if you have not already done so. If you have, reflect on the progress you have already made.
3. Take the next small step.
4. Read through and select your favorite affirmations from the *Inspiring Affirmations for Maxi Mom Success Worksheet* at the end of this chapter or create your own. Carry your favorite affirmations with you and read, listen to them or state them with confidence daily.
5. Use the *New You Checklist Worksheet* at the end of the chapter as a quick review of the tasks in this book and a checklist of skills that you have mastered.
6. Feel grateful that by creating the life of your dreams, both you and your child will greatly benefit.
7. Return to this book as needed and Repeat!

Celebrate the New You Exercises to Help Your Child

1. Work through the chapters in this book and model what you learn to your child. As you explore each chapter's age appropriate activities, slowly include the concepts in your daily routine, and introduce powerful success habits that can benefit your child for life.
2. Repeat!

INSPIRING AFFIRMATIONS FOR MAXI MOM SUCCESS

As you move forward there will be excitement, wonder, and many proud moments. At times there will also be obstacles and frustrations, but you can now handle them successfully and not let them derail your progress. Here are some affirmations to read and say out loud, that will remind you of all that you truly are and how wonderful your life can be.

YOU decide the path and the happiness in your life.

YOU DESIGN YOUR IDEAL LIFE!

1. I have the power of moms with dreams.
2. I know exactly what I have to do to achieve maximum success.
3. My dreams are much larger than my fears.
4. I am in charge of my emotions, desires, abilities and my life.
5. I feel confident, energetic, and powerful. I am on top of the world.
6. I will be successful today, tomorrow and always.
7. I am so grateful for this exact moment in time.
8. My mind and body are thriving and good health radiates throughout me.
9. I believe in myself and trust my inner conscience to be my guide.
10. I am creative, confident and able to successfully face any challenge.
11. Calmness surrounds me with every still breath that I take.
12. I see fear as the flame for my success and I will take massive action to succeed.

13. My power is within me. I learn from the past, live in the present and plan for the future.
14. I am great at solving problems and overcoming obstacles. I always find the best solutions.
15. I am unique. I feel great about being me. I am everything good.
16. Motivation comes to me easily and I also successfully motivate others.
17. I feel very successful in my life right now, especially as I work toward my future success.
18. I become more and more successful every day.
19. I breathe in relaxation. I breathe out stress over and over again.
20. Positivity is surrounding me and calming my soul.
21. I love being physically fit and at my ideal weight.
22. I love and respect my child as much as I love and respect myself.
23. I see the world through the eyes of my child and experience the joy of life.
24. Every muscle in my body is bathed in relaxation and sunshine.
25. I have integrity. I am reliable. I am confident. I do what I say.
26. I am strong and capable of doing anything I choose to do.
27. I am the creator of my thoughts and my life. I am designing the life of my dreams.
28. All my problems have a solution.
29. Each day I understand my purpose with greater clarity.
30. I attract success and positivity where ever I go.

31. I embrace only positive thoughts. I am free of negativity and blame.
32. All stress, fear and negativity are flowing away from my mind and body.
33. I am grateful for each and every moment of my life.
34. I will succeed in all that I do. Success is my natural state.
35. I am creating my ideal life full of passion, purpose and positivity.

THE NEW YOU CHECKLIST WORKSHEET

This checklist includes many of the tasks that are provided in the book. Review it frequently to ensure that you are using as many of the tips as you can to propel your life toward Maxi Mom Success. Include some of your own tips that you have discovered along the way. Return to this list often as you succeed and…

ENTER NEW AND EXCITING PHASES OF YOUR LIFE!

TIP/TASK	Y/N
Play the goodness game	
Evaluate your excuses	
Stop making excuses	
Be responsible for your actions	
Be grateful every day	
Use daily grateful reminders	
Know what you DO want	
Create, then review goals daily	
Evaluate your limiting beliefs	
Create positive beliefs	
Stop comparing to others	
Create a Victory List	
Review your Victory List often	
Create a Mind Map	
Create an Action Plan	
Pick a small step and begin!	
Take a set # of daily action steps	
Be accountable to someone else	
Connect with like-minded moms	
Delegate/Share/Swap/Reassess	
Complete daily reviews	
Replace bad habits with good	
Track how you spend your time	
Eliminate time wasters	

Finish incompletes	
Clean up messes	
Establish a routine	
Experiment to find what works	
Stay calm and be flexible	
Evaluate your fears	
Focus on positive outcomes	
Visualize great outcomes	
Make a list of fear-prints	
Dissolve fear into parts	
Practice on small fears first	
Weigh imagined fears vs. dreams	
Prepare for imagined fears	
Face fear and win!	
Play the tally your fear game	
Continue to learn daily	
ASK …ASK… ASK	
Research a topic	
Use the Brainstorm List	
Overcome an obstacle	
Celebrate your wins!	

Now that you have what you need to live your ideal life, what are you waiting for?

THE NEW YOU IS READY TO TAKE YOUR BREATH AWAY.

FROM ME TO YOU:

Congratulations on taking the first step to create the life you deserve for you and your family!

I believe everyone can benefit from inspiration, knowledge, and support. Every person has different circumstances and desires. Everyone is totally unique, so although there is no one process that works for everyone, the tips in this book *can* work for everyone. The key is adapting the process to your own unique situation. I believe in everyone! *I believe in you!*

ABOUT THE AUTHOR

Dar Batrowny is a child development specialist and the author of a developmental children's series entitled, *The Art of Early Learning Series, the Early Ed Series* and this inspirational and motivational book, entitled *The Power of Moms With Dreams.* She is the founder of the Maxi Mom Success System and World Child Development Day. She and her husband enjoy the New York State Finger Lakes Region. They have two wonderful children and a very fuzzy cat named Izzy. Dar loves educating and inspiring others to succeed and live the life of their dreams.

Learn more about Dar at https://www.amazon.com/author/dabatrowny.

Learn more about the Maxi Mom Success System, and how to be a Master Mom at http://beAmastermom.com.

Learn more about child development and her children's books at http://www.darbatrowny.com/ and http://liftAchild.com.

END

www.ingramcontent.com/pod-product-compliance
Lightning Source LLC
LaVergne TN
LVHW051551070426
835507LV00021B/2529